Cover
Designed and created by *Timeless Images,* Kemnay, Aberdeenshire, from an original photograph by Frazer Simpson

End-papers
The Union Buildings, Pretoria.
Courtesy *South African Tourism Board*

Ours the Harvest

A Life of Charles Murray

ALEX R SCOTT

Published by the
Charles Murray Memorial Fund

First published in Great Britain in 2003
by the Charles Murray Memorial Fund
34 Albyn Place, Aberdeen AB10 1 FW

A CIP catalogue record for this book is available from the British Library.
ISBN 0-9545682-1-4

Set in Bembo by XL Publishing Services, Tiverton

Printed in Great Britain by Polestar Wheatons Ltd.,
Hennock Road, Marsh Barton,
Exeter, Devon EX2 8RP

Cover created and illustrations processed
by *Timeless Images*, Kemnay, Aberdeenshire

To My Wife

in

Gratitude and Love

Charles Murray: *A Friend's Tribute*

He was a truly great man, strong in character, lovable in personality, imbued with a wisdom even beyond that which from time to time he allows to illuminate his poetry... to live constantly in the company of him and his associates was one long intellectual adventure, full of an endless variety of experience, of sound sense and boisterous fun, of serious scholarship and scientific discourse and anecdotal excursions.

Alex Keith
From *Transactions of the Buchan Club*
Vol. XVIII, Part 1

Contents

Acknowledgements

Without the assistance of many individuals and institutions at home and abroad this book would not have come into being. While Charles Murray himself would have disapproved of the project, his grandson, Kenneth M Walker, Edinburgh, gave it his blessing, providing in generous measure both material help and encouragement. Support was readily furnished also by Alford Heritage Centre Curator Robbie Gauld and by Alford Local History Group, under its efficient Secretary Margaret Black. First-hand particulars on my subject were added by the late William MacDonald of *Montgarrie Mill*, Charles F Spence of *The Forbes Arms Hotel*, and by Alford residents Jean Duncan, Chrissie Laing and Nan Sandison. John Bruce drew the admirable map of the village and Dr Gordon L Watt provided the fine photograph of the Murray grave. Except where otherwise attributed, the remaining photographs and textual quotations appear by kind permission of the Charles Murray Estate.

Researchers interested in Charles Murray must place themselves under deep obligation to Manuscripts Division, the National Library of Scotland, which houses a rich archive of material. Staff at Aberdeen City and County Libraries – notably Alford branch – also proved invariably helpful, as did: the Special Libraries and Archives of Aberdeen University; the Elphinstone Institute under Dr Ian Russell; Aberdeen and York City Art Galleries; the National Library of South Africa, Cape Town Division; University of the Witwatersrand Library, Johannesburg; Documentation Centre, Department of Defence, Pretoria; the South African Tourism Board, Pretoria; the South African High Commission, London.

For help in financing publication of this volume, I have to thank the trustees of the Charles Murray Memorial Fund, under Chairman James A D Michie who not only furnished the Foreword but, together with fellow-trustee Dr Colin Milton, took time to read and make valuable observations on the manuscript.

I must voice appreciation too of the services of Stuart Coyle of *Polestar Wheatons Ltd, Exeter*, who skilfully saw the work through the stages of production. The processing of illustrations and development of the cover design were in the capable hands of Frazer Simpson of *Timeless Images*,

Kemnay, Aberdeenshire, who brought to the tasks technical expertise, artistry and enthusiasm. To him also I offer my thanks.

My deepest gratitude, however, must be reserved for my wife, Norma, who has given unstintingly of her time and proficiency throughout the long birth-pangs of this biography, turning flawed script into faultless floppy disc. The imperfections of the undertaking are mine.

Alex R Scott
Alford, October 2003

Foreword

It could be said that most of us take our prose and poetry from the printed page and savour their delights without too much enquiry into the life histories of their writers and composers. Some works are such that they stand on their own entire of themselves; others are clouded by the personal excesses of their authors to such an extent that one is lost to the other. It is good when man and artist are inseparable and each can be interpreted in the light of the other as creativity rises out of the deep wells of experience. So it is with Charles Murray and *Hamewith*. They are as Bennachie is to the Vale of Alford, conjoined, the icons at the core of all he ever wrote. He had a warm respect for the people of the Vale and a genuine understanding of their whimsical approach to life; above all he took pride in the tribal Doric which he found peerless in its expressivity of country character and rural lore.

Personal choice rather than fate led to him spending twenty-three years of his working life in the service, first of all, of the Transvaal and then in the new Union of South Africa. He rose to become Secretary for Public Works of the latter and such were the range and quality of his work and the excellence of his service that in a professional sense, he may be regarded as one of the founding fathers of the Union. For this alone he merits permanent recognition away beyond the honours conferred upon him by university and Crown.

Unaccountably, no full scale biography of Charles Murray has appeared – until now. *Ours the Harvest* is thus greatly to be welcomed. Written as a labour of love, it brings man and poet, home and abroad, into synchronism in the most felicitous manner.

Hamewith is out of Africa; Africa *was* Alford for, in an emotional sense, Charles Murray never ever really left home. Out of meticulous research *Ours the Harvest* brings this to bear so tellingly and authoritatively that, even now, it is a valuable companion volume to the sharply focused, life-affirming work itself.

James A D Michie
Chairman
Charles Murray Memorial Fund

Introduction

Scots settle abroad, alleges the cynic, because their homeland is best viewed from afar. However hotly that may be disputed, there is assuredly none more patriotic than the expatriate Scot. The subject of this portrait is a case in point. Charles Murray (1864–1941), known also as 'Hamewith' from the title of his first public collection of verse, spent almost all his working life in South Africa as pioneer, prospector, public servant. There, intense love for his birthplace, the Aberdeenshire village of Alford, drew from memory the scenes, the characters, the language of home which furnished almost the entire substance of his 'sangs'. To style them 'poetry' was, in his view, to overrate them.

On his death, it was the hope of his widow, Edith Emma (*née* Rogers) that the story of his life would be told by someone personally acquainted with him. Regrettably, the attempt was never made. So extensive were his travels, so diverse his activities, that no individual could have first-hand knowledge of every aspect. Fewer and fewer are those who, looking back to their early years, can recollect encounters with the man himself. The would-be chronicler is, therefore, heavily dependent upon contemporary accounts and records from many sources: official material, family photographs and memorabilia, memoirs of segments of a long and varied life.

One of those near-contemporary accounts, published 1943, was that of fellow-Scot and junior colleague in South Africa, Charles Christie, whose monograph *Some memories of Charles Murray and a few of his friends,* a valuable quarry of information, raised further complications in addressing this particular subject. 'Murray's biographer,' he wrote, 'will have to deal not only with the lights and shades of temperament and character, the problem of all biographers, but will have to make his account with the fact that there were half-a-dozen Charles Murrays and that anything said of one of them has often to be qualified by reference to the others. Of those known to the world, there was the Murray of the administrative competence and resolute commonsense but there was the Peter Pan Murray; there was the artist and the poet; there was the dyed-in-the-wool Tory with his Radical notions and his sympathy with the under-dog; there was the devotee of "laughter and the love of friends." … this much may be said of the man; it was not what he did but what he was that counted with the generation that knew him; in that crowd of very capable people there were those who had bigger and more spectacular things to do, but there was no bigger man.'

Some five years ago, when preparing to deliver a talk on Charles Murray to a gathering of the latter's fellow-villagers, the present writer was sternly admonished by the then Curator of the local Heritage Centre, Robbie Gauld: "Spik nae ill o' Charlie Murray afore Alford folk!" The advice proved needless: no 'ill' came to light; not one critical voice was heard amidst the chorus of acclamation. Not one? Candour requires acknowledgement of a single faction, comprising the celebrated Scots poet Hugh MacDiarmid (Christopher Murray Grieve) and his advocates, who dismissed Charles Murray's writing as negligible.

No purpose would be served by blowing on the embers of a fire long dead. Suffice it to say that Hugh MacDiarmid, justifiably, took himself seriously, while Charles Murray, part-time poet, seldom did. He was without pretension, far too intent for the most part upon Scots figures in the North-east landscape they shared to dwell upon self. Charged – by his *alter ego* – with wasting time penning inconsequential verses, he responds:

> Nae care hae I, nor wish to speel
> Parnassus' knowe, for mony a chiel
> Has tint his time, his life as weel,
> > To claim a bit o't:
> I only crave a wee bit biel'
> > Near han' the fit o't.

It is the present writer's aim, in the pages that follow, to retrace as nearly as he can the road that led Charles Murray in the late 19th century from the rural peace of an Aberdeenshire parish and the clatter of Aberdeen's cobbled streets, through the din, dirt and stench of boom-town Johannesburg, city of gold, to a succession of key roles in the emerging Union of South Africa and eventually, with honours royal and academic to his name, *hamewith* – homewards, back to his Alford roots. Sixty years and more after his death it is not too soon to tell his story.

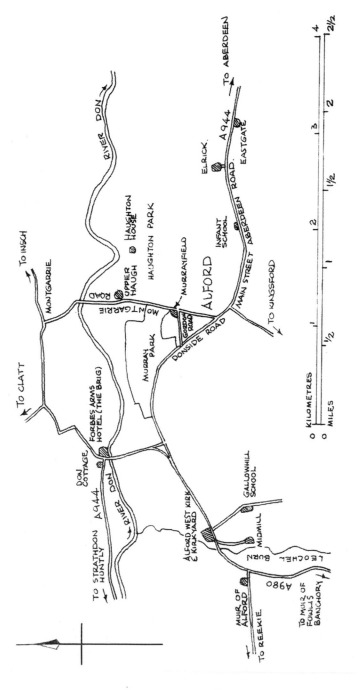

Places about the Aberdeenshire village of Alford linked to Charles Murray

Map drawn by John Bruce

CHAPTER 1

Birth, Parentage, Schooling

'When we were loons at school'
The Ae Reward

Nor hail nor sleet, nor tropic heat can vex him now. In the lee of Alford West Kirk, his ashes rest. Charles Murray – the poet Hamewith – is back among his own folk, back in his beloved Donside at the close of a life intensely lived and rich in achievement.

At 6 am on 28 September 1864, at *Eastgate*, a trim but unremarkable single-storeyed cottage, a mile on the Aberdeen side of present-day Alford, Charles Murray was born. A plaque identifies the birthplace. His parents, Peter Murray, master plough- and cart-wright of *Midmill* and his wife, Margaret (*née* Robbie) of Deeside, already had a daughter, Sarah, approaching two years of age. Sadly their third child, Peter, did not survive infancy but died on 18 March 1867, aged 10½ months.

Margaret Murray herself did not long outlive her baby son. In January 1868, at the age of 30, she succumbed to a wasting disease, identified as *phthisis*. This may have predisposed her son Charles to the bronchial weakness from which he suffered throughout his life.

Charles, for his part, writing in middle-age to his son, 16-year-old William, mentions the supposedly fragile state of his own boyhood health, setting it in the context of the abiding bond between his father and himself. 'My father and I,' he attests, 'were always very good chums although he gave me many and many a hiding. I suppose we were thrown together a good deal especially in the winter time when I could not go to school... He had the extra anxiety about me because I was considered delicate and not able to take on hard manual labour... '

Enforced absence from school, a ban on strenuous physical effort and access to carpentry tools perhaps directed the young lad's energies towards woodwork. Here he must have shown some aptitude for he is listed among the top prize-winners in a national fretwork competition run by a boys' magazine. Even in his 60th year he harks back to those teenage days. In a letter to his son, now in his mid-twenties, Charles

Eastgate, Aberdeen Road, Alford, birthplace of Charles Murray

muses: 'I wonder what we could do with my fret-cutter. It wouldn't be any use to you. Perhaps we will hear of some country boy who would like it. It filled in many long winter days for me.'

Alleged sickliness did not, however, deter him from engaging in schoolboy horseplay with adversaries heavier than himself, as he recounts in another letter to William. '(Your) grandfather,' he reveals, 'was a great wrestler when at school and (wrestling) was one thing which as a small boy always let me in amongst the big boys. It was a sort of collar and elbow wrestling. We held each other by the neck of the jacket and it was a case of footwork... I had a special trip which I discovered and kept to myself and which brought down many a bigger boy.'

Nevertheless, reports of his frailty persisted. One was aired as late as 1960 in a BBC radio programme on the poet. Margaret McCreadie, daughter of his teacher at Gallowhill School, voiced what for her can only have been hearsay, Charles being close on 19 and an apprentice in Aberdeen before she was born. She stated that he was 'a very delicate boy... and very, very mischievous.' His subsequent career gave the lie to the first, but did nothing to efface the name he had for skylarking that pursued him even to the corridors and chambers of the South African Parliament.

Margaret Murray (*née* Robbie) of Birse, Deeside, (1838–68), mother of Sarah, Charles and Peter

Charles never knew his maternal grandfather, Charles Robbie, a woodsawyer of Birse, Deeside. He had died in 1853, eight years before the marriage of his daughter, Margaret. By contrast, grandmother Jane Robbie (*née* Christie) was to play a significant role in the lives of her grandchildren, the adolescent Sarah and Charles Murray. She must have been a remarkable woman, a woman of wisdom and tenacity. Unable at the time of her marriage either to read or to write, she resolved that any children of the union should not be similarly disadvantaged. Accordingly she embarked on teaching first herself and subsequently her children to do both.

Jane Robbie (*née* Christie) of Birse, Deeside (1817–98),
maternal grandmother of Charles Murray

Her foresight brought its own reward. One of her daughters, Mrs N Scott, who had settled in New Zealand, wrote to her nephew Charles, perhaps early in 1921 on hearing of the honour accorded him by the University of Aberdeen in recognition of his contribution to Scottish letters. 'I always say,' his aunt maintained, 'it was from your mother you inherited your genius for poetry. I can remember your mother as a girl. Mother used to say that Maggie had a mania for making rhyme. She was a very clever girl for I can remember when she was taken from school on account of our parents not being able to pay for the three of us. The teacher said how sorry she was for she was the best in the school… she left her mantle for her son who has worn it wisely and well.'

Peter Murray, father of Sarah and Charles, came of farming folk. His parents – Peter Murray, senior, farmer and miller, and Agnes (*née* Jeffrey)

Charles Murray's grandfather, Peter Murray, Snr., farmer and miller, *Midmill*, Alford, died 13 November 1884, aged 86

– had tenancy of *Midmill Farm* by the Leochel Burn, no distance from Alford West Parish Church. Peter and Agnes Murray and her mother-in-law, also of *Midmill* (great-grandmother of Charles and Sarah) have their own claim to celebrity.

In 1854, while the pupils were on holiday, there came to Gallowhill School, two artists: John Phillip of Oldmeldrum and his friend, Aberdeen-born John Stirling – 'gey fellows'(scamps) in the recollection of Peter Murray, the poet's father. Their purpose in visiting Alford, apart from relaxation, was to execute studies for a series of *genre* paintings entitled *Scottish Presbyterians in a Country Parish Church*. The setting for Stirling's *The Sermon* and Phillip's *Collecting the Offering* is Alford West Parish Church, but the essays were done in the schoolroom of Gallowhill. Phillip's sitters included the Rev. Hugh McConnach (predecessor of Charles Murray's schoolmaster – Anthony McCreadie), flanked in the painting by the two Mrs Murrays, grandmother of Charles on his right, great-grandmother on his left. The original *Collecting the Offering* now hangs in York Art Gallery. In Stirling's *The Sermon*, a 'Peter Murray' is identified among the congregation, but it is unclear to whom the name

Collecting the Offering in a Scottish Kirk – John Phillip
Courtesy York City Art Gallery

refers: almost certainly the youthful man in front who could be the poet's father-to-be aged 20; or, less likely, the older man behind, possibly the poet's grandfather-to-be at the age of 56.

Etching by an unknown hand of John Stirling's painting *Scottish Presbyterians in a Country Church – The Sermon*   *Present owner untraced*

The year 1861 was another memorable in the lives of Peter and Agnes Murray. Within the space of a month they saw a son and daughter married: first Peter on May 30 at *Elrick*; and then Sarah on June 27 at *Midmill*. The marriage of Peter and Margaret was cut tragically short when after only six summers she died, leaving him at 34 with a living to earn and two children, aged five and three, to bring up.

Providentially, help was at hand. Mary Robbie, his late wife's younger sister, at once assumed responsibility for her niece and nephew and for managing household affairs. She remained with her brother-in-law until her dying day. Her last resting place in Alford West Churchyard, alongside that of Peter Murray, his wife and infant son, is like theirs marked by a cross. It bears the inscription:

ERECTED BY
PETER MURRAY
IN REMEMBRANCE OF
MARY ROBBIE

HIS FAITHFUL FRIEND AND HOUSEKEEPER
FOR FORTY-SEVEN YEARS
DIED AT MURRAYFIELD ALFORD
APRIL 21ST 1915 AGED 75 YEARS

Much later, Charles Murray was to say that, in all their time together, he never once heard his father and his aunt exchange an angry word.

Peter Murray, seen here (c. 1868) with his children Charles and Sarah, and his late wife's sister, Mary Robbie, who devoted her life to their care

The Murray children, then, despite the untimely loss of their mother, were not denied a stable and loving home, even if material possessions were scant. In due course Charles was enrolled at the Boys' School on the eastern approach to the village, where his teacher was a James Todd. There it was that Charles first met fellow-pupil James Tocher, a close contemporary, who was to distinguish himself in divers scientific fields and, many years later, re-enter Charles Murray's life.

Their early acquaintanceship was recalled on 29 October 1925, when Charles, on retiring from his life-work in South Africa, was honoured by a company of admirers at a ceremony in Aberdeen Art Gallery. In recognition of his contribution to Scots poetry, he was presented with his portrait in oils, painted by G. Fiddes Watt, RSA. Chairman of the organising committee was none other than that old schoolmate – now Dr James F Tocher – who recollected in his introductory remarks that 'for an all too brief period we had as "wee loonies" the same experiences of childhood. We were at that time too wee to be "lickit" but I do not doubt we often deserved it.'

Subsequently, in his obituary of Charles Murray, published (1941) in the *Aberdeen University Review,* Dr Tocher claimed that they both 'attended the same little school at the east end of the village and both left that school in 1872.' Yet the only document relating to Charles to survive from those days is a combined invoice and 'abstract of Attendance and

Sarah and Charles Murray with their uncle, Charles Robbie (c. 1871)
Yerbury, Edinburgh

Marks' for 6 months in the elegant copperplate of their teacher James Todd. Dated 18 July 1873, it records 239 attendances out of a possible 255 over 6 months; awards Charles 87% for both Reading and Grammar, 81% for Bible, 78% for Arithmetic and 74% for conduct; and submits to Mr P Murray a bill 'To Teaching Charles 4 wks' in the amount of – one shilling and four pence.

Gallowhill School, Wellhouse Brae, Alford, where Charles Murray had his post-elementary schooling   *Author's photograph*

The next reference to Charles in an educational context appears in the pages of the Admission Register of Alford Gallowhill Public School, on Wellhouse Brae, a mile west of present-day Alford. There he is listed as Number 224 with the 'Date of Admission or Re-admission' given as '2.4.77' No prior admission date is traceable, but it is possible that earlier Admission Registers have not survived. His 'Exact Date of Birth' is given – wrongly – as '2.9.64'.

Be that as it may, Charles was extremely fortunate in his teacher, Edinburgh University graduate Anthony McCreadie, MA, an Ayrshire man, who served Gallowhill and the community over many years,

Anthony McCreadie, M.A., F.E.I.S. (1845–1930), Charles Murray's
schoolmaster at *Gallowhill School*, Alford
Fred W Hardie, Aberdeen

earning both their confidence and respect. He recognised and encouraged the gifts latent in his young pupil but modestly attributed their
flowering more to heredity than to education.

In the years up to 1880, when his school-days came to an end, the
name of Charles Murray appears only once in Gallowhill School Log
Book, a week-by-week record of noteworthy events. The entry for 2
December 1878 reads: 'Charles Murray brought a certificate from Dr
Smith that there was no danger of infection and was allowed to re-enter
his classes.'

Schooldays over, the regard in which Charles held Mr McCreadie
warmed into life-long friendship. Indeed, until a school-house was available, Mr McCreadie had lodged with the Murray family. The death in
December 1899 of Mrs McCreadie, formerly a teacher at Gallowhill,

drew from Charles a touching and elegantly penned letter of condolence in which he admitted to the widower that, while he had as a schoolboy viewed him with something akin to dread, he had always found Mrs McCreadie much more approachable.

Acknowledging a letter of congratulations from Mr McCreadie on his honorary doctorate from the University of Aberdeen nearly forty years after leaving school, Charles writes: 'I was very glad to get your letter. As I sit down to answer it, the old Gallowhill days crowd back. I can see the gean trees, the hedge, the dyke and the well and I can see Sandy Anderson of Westside harrying a bike (bees' nest) on the top of one of Adam Taylor's dykes and hear his remark when a bee stung him. He hesitated in doubt for a minute and then said, "Oh dam't, I dinna swall" and into the bike again.'

Dear old pals; Charles (*left*) and his cousin Jack Murray
hamming it up as schoolboys (c. 1879)

Three years later, in June 1923, another of Mr McCreadie's letters gave rise to an account by Charles of a chance encounter in South Africa between himself and 'an old schoolfellow – "feel (witless) Sammy Allan"' on a train bound for East London. With a sense of the dramatic, Charles recounts: '... the afternoon of the second day out (from Cape Town) a burly, red-faced, white-haired man entered my carriage very excited, called me by name and shook me wildly by the hand. It was "feel Sammy" though I would not have known him. He must have had some substantial qualities as he was a Sergeant-Major under Kitchener in the Boer War. He has been hotel keeping for years, steady and prosperous, but still with the daft look in his eyes. I heard that in his bar he had over 50 clocks which sounds a bit "feel" though there is no reason why a man should not collect clocks as well as snuff-boxes or pictures. His wife was with him, a capable looking, intelligent woman. As far as I could gather, she was a widow and he got her by advertisement. She told me she had a sister who married into the Welsh peerage! It is rather funny to think of Sammy being connected even by marriage with the peerage.'

Some 70 years on from those earliest Alford schooldays, Dr. Tocher, a rhymer himself, prompted two of Hamewith's *Last Poems* : the high-spirited *J.F.T.*, written in 1937 to mark the presentation to Tocher of his portrait; and *Ae Year's Bairns* (1940), a humorously philosophical wartime view of life's approaching end for two who shared 1864 as the year of their birth.

In two of his best-loved and most recited poems, *The Whistle* and *It Wasna His Wyte*, Charles, with – for the most part – affectionate memories of schooldays and an artist's eye for detail, captures the absorption of two schoolboys in their surroundings and pursuits. In both poems the "maister" or "Dominie" is portrayed as a natural enemy, a vindictive or predatory killjoy:

But the snaw it stopped the herdin' an' the winter brocht him dool,
When in spite o' hacks an' chilblains he was shod again for school;
He couldna sough the catechis nor pipe the rule o' three,
He was keepit in an' licket when the ither loons got free;
But he aften played the truant – 'twas the only thing he played,
For the maister brunt the whistle that the wee herd made!

★ ★ ★ ★ ★ ★ ★ ★

He tried on his taes to creep ben till his seat,
    But the snuffy aul' Dominie saw,
Sneckit there in his dask like a wyver that waits
    For a flee in his wob on the wa';
He tell't o' his tum'le, but fat was the eese
    Wi' the mannie in sic an ill teen,
An' fat was a wap wi' a spainyie or tag
    To hands that were hard as a steen?

High-spirited and self-confessedly "lazy", Charles would have earned and endured his portion of punishment at the hands of Mr McCreadie, but the boy would not have overstepped the mark. Money was not plentiful in the Murray household. Charles knew what it was to go barefoot in patched clothes. He had, in consequence, too high a regard for his father, too great an awareness of the sacrifices made to keep him at school, for him to scamp his studies.

Although prone, even as an adult, to spelling errors and faulty sentence construction in English, it is likely that Charles studied Latin at Gallowhill, for it was taught there, and taught well, judging by the comments by Her Majesty's Inspectors of Schools on their regular visits. A knowledge of Latin would, in part, explain the inclusion in his published verse of eleven versions in Scots from Horace and Virgil. In his letters he was to pass some shrewd observations on the style of the former which revealed a critical acumen that he always disclaimed.

The fact that his poetry is written almost exclusively in Scots was, he said, neither deliberate nor accidental but inevitable. Scots was his birthright, the voice of his imagination. He admitted that he was torn between the claims of the Doric, tongue of his family, his schoolmates, his fellow villagers, and the standard English expected of him in the classroom. This perplexity persisted when, aged 16, he started work in Aberdeen and had to frame in English all communication with his employers.

His love of the Doric was early instilled and nurtured by his father, himself a singer and adept at verse, but verse too "pointed" to be published. He it was who urged his son to be alive to "our sappy words and pithy phrases" and to employ them. Charles was a receptive pupil. His poems abound in apt and telling expressions. A few suffice to illustrate the point. In *The Braw Lass* we chuckle over "The gowkit fee'd 'oman" that ... "Cam' clyte in the midden..." Sight of Isie in the poem of that name has "The baillie's hairt... duntin' aneth his sark", while fortune favours Belcanny, anti-hero of *There's Aye A Something*: "his boolie rowes weel..."

An artist in words as well as in wood, Peter Murray presently relinquished his role of village carpenter and his tenancy of *Eastgate* to take up employment as "Ground Officer" of the Haughton Estate, owned by the Farquharson family, largest land-holders in the locality. His duties included liaising between estate owner and tenants, ensuring that the latter's needs were met and that maintenance work on the estate was carried out.

The post entitled the holder to estate accommodation, in this case a substantial granite dwelling-house, named *Upperhaugh*, set in extensive grounds, on the road between Alford and Montgarrie. To *Upperhaugh*, then, moved the Murray household: Peter, his two children Sarah and Charles, and his sister-in-law and housekeeper, Mary Robbie.

Peter Murray and Mary Robbie, his sister-in-law, in the garden of *Upperhaugh*, the house they shared until his retirement

Pen and ink drawing of *Barra Castle*, Oldmeldrum,
executed by Charles Murray, aged 16

Pen and ink drawing of a fishing fleet
by Charles Murray (c. 1880)

Peter Murray held the position of Ground Officer for many years, serving the Farquharsons capably and faithfully and earning their esteem and appreciation. When extreme age compelled him to retire, the Farquharsons expressed their gratitude by having a house built where he could live out his remaining years. This handsome haven was given the name *Murrayfield*.

His successor as Ground Officer was Joseph Watson and it is to one of the latter's daughters, Mrs Jean Duncan of Alford, that the writer is indebted for this account of one of the pranks that young Charles Murray would get up to as a schoolboy living at *Upperhaugh*. Always a bit of a jester, he gave a new slant to the phrase "cap and bells".

High up on the kitchen wall of *Upperhaugh*, in common with many such multi-roomed houses, especially where domestic help was employed, hung a row of bells, each linked by a wire and a "pull" to a different room to summon attendance. Returning blithely from school, Charles would fling his bonnet forcibly at the bells to set them all jangling, doubtless to the annoyance of his Aunt Mary.

Apart from providing any such indoor entertainment, *Upperhaugh* was — and remains — the sort of house that would delight any lover of nature, girt about as it is by gently swelling hills, rolling farmland, deep woods and all their denizens. Close by, silent and unseen, forming the northern boundary of the Parish of Alford, the River Don traces a sinuous course between low grassy banks. Amid such surroundings Charles, consciously or subconsciously, was storing those images of nature or humankind, upon which in distant places he would largely draw in the writing of his poems. His ear and his sensitivities too were becoming attuned to the nuances of the language, the cadences of North-east speech that bring his scenes and characters graphically into being. From classroom study of old Scots writers, particularly Allan Ramsay, Robert Fergusson and Robert Burns, came the realisation that the vernacular was a fit vehicle for serious poetic composition and the obvious medium for his own essays in verse:

> O for a day at the Hint o' Hairst,
> Wi' the craps weel in an' stackit,
> When the farmer steps thro' the corn-yard,
> An' counts a' the rucks he's thackit:
> *The Hint o' Hairst*

CHAPTER 2

Apprenticeship

'Then mak' my bed in Aiberdeen'
"Aiberdeen Awa'!"

As schooldays drew to a close, Charles and, doubtless, his father, perhaps his teacher also, would have had his future training and subsequent occupation increasingly in mind. Whatever option had been chosen, it is beyond question that Charles Murray would have excelled: he was that kind of lad, obedient to his respected father's precept: "Always do your best."

A career choice was made. With effect "from and after the tenth day of January Eighteen hundred and eighty-one," Charles Murray, three and a half months into his 17th year, found himself bound as apprentice "for the space of Five full and complete years" to the Firm of Walker and Beattie, Land Surveyors in Aberdeen, with offices first at 91 Union Street and subsequently at 3 Golden Square. It seems to have been a mutually beneficial arrangement. For the privilege of thus placing his son (wageless throughout), Peter Murray had to pay a premium of £50 as well as keeping the boy. 'I wonder yet how he managed,' wrote Charles, with that understated admiration characteristic of the North-east.

The time came to enter upon his apprenticeship. Dressed in new moleskin trousers, cocked bonnet and ample neckcloth against the piercing cold of a particularly severe winter and carrying basic necessities such as a bag of meal and "some other non-perishable comestibles", Charles left Alford for Aberdeen. He did not travel alone. With him were his father and his 18-year-old sister, Sarah, whose artistic talents – shared by her brother – were to secure her a place at Gray's School of Art, Aberdeen, on its opening in 1884. Nor were the pair destined to dwell among strangers in a strange land. Initially at least, according to the 1881 census, they were living with their late mother's mother, widowed Grannie Jane Robbie, aged 64, at 25 Broomhill Place, Old Machar. On six shillings a week, which was all that Charles could contribute to the household budget, the fare must have been plain and creature comforts few. Writing to his close friends, the Walker family, some 20 years later, he recalls Spartan conditions: 'I am reading *Noctes Ambrosianae* just now which reminds me of one winter when, living with my granny, I borrowed your copy of this and used to wrap myself up in the blankets without undressing and laugh myself warm over it.'

This accommodation was not a permanent arrangement. Although Charles was later – nearly 40 years later – to declare in verses entitled *"Aiberdeen Awa'!"* –

> O pair for fouchen here wi' heat
> I weary for the wind an' weet
> An' drivin' drift in Union Street
> tae th' Duke to Bauly Law.

this was merely a courteous compliment to his hosts, the Aberdeen University Club of South Africa, welcoming an Associate Member to their ranks. In reality, he heeded medical advice and sought lodgings barely four miles from the city centre in the balmier air of Cults village, where his congenital chest complaint troubled him less. The climate there proved not only healthier but more convivial. Writing in the *Leopard* magazine in March 1978, Dr Nan Shepherd, the Aberdeen poet, novelist and scholar, recalled her mother's accounts of meetings of the Cults Glee Society in one another's houses. When her house was the venue, young Charles Murray, caught up in story-telling, would lose track of time, until at 2 am his hostess would gently prevail upon him to go home, allowing the family to retire to bed. In later life Charles was to recollect with affection the kindness of the Shepherd household.

Charles proved himself an apt and diligent apprentice. From his Candidate's Circular, submitted prior to his election as an associate member of The Institution of Civil Engineers, some idea may be gained of the range and variety of his training and experience. In addition to all the regular and general work of a civil engineering and surveying company, he attended two sessions at Robert Gordon's (Technical) College, Aberdeen, obtaining certificates in drawing, building construction, applied mechanics and elementary electricity. He also undertook private classes for mathematics and classes in steam, electricity, mechanics and mechanical engineering. Whatever his ultimate ambition, he was clearly intent on thorough preparation in a wide range of disciplines.

Apprentice surveyors (c. 1885): Charles Murray is standing second right

Discipline in another sense featured prominently throughout his years in Aberdeen. Early in January 1883, at the age of 18, he enrolled in the 1st Aberdeenshire Engineer Volunteer Corps, formed as recently as April 1878, from the 1st Aberdeen Rifle Volunteers. What prompted him to this move can only be conjectured. Were there some among his particular friends − including from 1882 a George Walker − who, led by a sense of comradeship and adventure, persuaded him to enlist? Current newspaper reports, while generally playing down their gravity, kept before their readers − in Aberdeen as elsewhere − instances of inflammatory speeches and agitation by Boer nationalists, resentful of British imperial aspirations across South Africa. If Charles even then harboured thoughts of a future in "the colonies", he perhaps deemed it prudent to equip himself to meet all contingencies. It is probable that he already had some knowledge of guns, gained from his father whose occupation as Ground Officer would have required it. Indeed Peter Murray was something of a marksman. Charles relates how his father, blinded in his right eye when a tack he was driving flew up and struck him, taught himself to shoot placing the gun-stock on his left-shoulder. Whatever motives impelled Charles to enrol, it is certainly the case, as his subsequent career and his writing demonstrate, that bearing arms had a powerful appeal for him.

Corporal Charles Murray, First Aberdeen Engineer Volunteers, (c. 1884)

With his customary fervour he threw himself into Infantry Drill and mastering the elements of Military and Field Engineering. In a letter to his 17-year-old son, who was himself poised to enter the forces in the early stages of World War I, Charles recalls his own volunteer days: 'I… used to shoot a bit. One year I earned my marksman's badge, but it cost five shillings to get it put on my sleeve and I could never raise the money… (George Walker) and I once won the prize for the best kept tent in camp and very proud we were of it and had it photographed.'

George W S Walker, lifelong friend of Charles Murray, (c. 1887)

A corporal in mid-1887, he had by 3 January 1888, been made up to sergeant as evidenced in a testimonial furnished by one of his lecturers at Robert Gordon's College, Frank G Ogilvie, who happened also to be a Captain in the 1st Aberdeenshire Engineer Volunteer Corps. Having praised him for the "diligence, intelligence and success with which he pursued his studies," Captain Ogilvie went on to pay tribute to his expertise and qualities of character in a military context. He stated: "I regarded... Sergeant Charles Murray as a most efficient member of the Corps. He possesses in a remarkable degree the faculty of getting men to work at their best and in the best spirit; in the examination for proficiency in Military Engineering, he obtained the highest number of marks in his batch; and he was one of the most active members of the squad selected for Military Surveying." He concluded in a post-script: "I cordially recommend Mr Murray as a thoroughly competent and most agreeable assistant and as discreet and entirely trustworthy when placed in charge of work."

Charles stood tall in the estimation not only of his officers but also of the other ranks. "An Old Sapper", writing in response to an item relating to Charles headed "An Aberdonian in Johannesburg" in the Aberdeen *Evening Express* of 17 January 1896, took the paper to task for an oversight: "... you omit to mention Mr Charles Murray's services to the volunteer cause while in Aberdeen. In fact, he was one of the most energetic members that the Engineer Volunteers have ever had, either at drill or at any of their social functions, and equally at home either at Chatham or Culter." (Training camps were held annually at these locations.) "When the Rifles" (the 1st Aberdeen Rifle Volunteers) "had their last camp at Culter, Mr Murray was in charge of the detachment of Engineer Volunteers at the bridge" (the temporary structure erected to demonstrate military engineering skills) "and was one of the number who got pitched into the Dee by the overturning of one of the barrel piers owing to a heavy spate in the river."

The correspondent goes on to refer to a pamphlet entitled *As You Were*, largely the work of Charles Murray, "which was sold in large numbers at the Volunteer Bazaar." Held in the Music Hall, Aberdeen, over the four days immediately preceding Christmas 1887, the bazaar, under the patronage of Her Majesty the Queen, raised the sum of £1931 2s 6d towards the hire of drill-rooms and arms depots, costs which had to be defrayed by the three volunteer corps themselves – Artillery, Engineers and Gordon Highlanders.

As You Were is attributed to "Sappers Trigger and Trench", and consists of prose and verse, illustrations and mock advertisements. Much of it has topical or private reference; so the allusions are lost upon us. Charles Murray does not put his name to any of it, but the text is hand-written and beyond question his neat and regular script. For its whimsicality and deft rhymes, this double-limerick might just be laid at his door:

> There was a young lady of Culter
> Who thought a red coat would just suit'er;
> Her chest was all right
> But she wasn't the height
> And we didn't know where we could pult'er.

> Then up spoke the piccolo flulter –
> His civil profession's a soulter –
> "Our new Bugle-Major
> I'm sure will engage her
> To play in the band on a toolter."

In concluding, the writer to the newspaper indicated the regard in which Charles was held. "He was very popular with his brother sergeants, and before leaving this country was entertained by them to supper, and presented with a valuable field-glass as a token of their esteem.

'It's a mercy we're a' spared', was his remark on coming out of the river at Culter, and that he may long be able to say, this is the earnest wish of his volunteer friends, and of

AN OLD SAPPER"

At the age of 23, then, Charles Murray had already established a reputation for industry, professionalism, inter-personal skills and reliability. This last is further attested by his rating on discharge from the Volunteer Corps. On the eve – literally – of his departure for South Africa, he requested to be struck off the Muster Roll of the First Aberdeenshire

Engineers after six years' service. In each of these years, from 9 January 1883 to 15 December 1888, he had been "returned as an Efficient in the Annual Return of the Corps".

His literary interests were not confined to compiling *As You Were*. Throughout the 1880's he kept a commonplace book in which he entered verse or prose – "other men's flowers" – that appealed to him. Books of poems in the possession of the Walker family may have provided material for transcription. Many years later he referred to it in terms that suggested he had it still.

Socialising in Cults, serving in the Volunteers and pursuing his love of literature by no means exhausted his extra-curricular activities. He had become captain of a football club; taken up cricket and, though not much of a batsman, 'bowled a bit'; and was asked to play rugby for the County but stayed loyal to the club he started with. Three years running he played for the City team against the University. 'I got my place,' he admitted to his son, 'just through hard work, good tackling and always keeping on the ball' – tactics he adopted in his professional career too.

In 1888 – his 'last year in Aberdeen' – by sheer force of personality, but not in any self-assertive way, Charles – the son of a former village-carpenter and unable to cite a lofty pedigree – was accepted as more than an equal into the rather exclusive Aberdeen Boating Club, plying the waters of the River Dee. He recalls that he 'was in the senior crew that lost the championship of the Dee for the first time in 20 years.' Through the boating club there developed a friendship that led in 1889 to a business partnership in distant Johannesburg.

Although the period of his apprenticeship was fully and variously occupied, Charles would have found time and means to visit Alford, if not regularly at least occasionally. He had tales to swap with his father and friendships to keep in repair. It was not only talk, however, that drew him back to village and howe. As lovers of his poems will know, he had – despite his disclaimers – a well-attuned ear, not for words alone but for music too. His father, it should be remembered, was a singer as well as a versifier and instilled in him a knowledge and an appreciation of the songs of the North-east. Music, then, added to the enjoyment of his visits home, but music in which he played an active part as the following reveals.

Writing in 1914 to Alexander Mackie, Editor of the *Aberdeen University Review*, Charles relates how memories, all but lost, had been vividly brought back by a letter from an old friend currently overseas, John Michie, whose parents' home on Donside had been the setting for evenings of home-brewed entertainment.

'John and I had many ploys in the strath in the middle eighties,' Charles recalls. 'I was very fond of the whole family. The old couple were as fine a pair as you could wish and many a happy night I've had fiddling and dancing in their kitchen. I had almost forgot that I once had a strong bow-han' until John asked if I ever fiddled now.'

Such recollections may well have been the genesis of his early poem *Winter* which opened his short-lived, 1893 volume, *A Handful of Heather*, but which reappeared in the first and subsequent editions of *Hamewith*. The poet not only creates a graphic contrast between wild, hostile exterior and cosy, welcoming interior, but also shows a knowledge of the technique of fiddle playing and the names of composers of fiddle music:

> Syne Sandy, gantin', raxes doon
> His fiddle fae the skelf aboon,
> Throws by the bag, an' souffs a tune,
> > Screws up a string,
> Tries antics on the shift, but soon
> > Starts some auld spring.

★   ★   ★   ★   ★

> An opening chord wi' lang upbow
> The fiddler strikes, syne gently now
> Glides into some Strathspey by Gow,
> > Or Marshall't may be;
> The dancers lichtly needle thro'
> > Rab sets to Leebie.

The last but one stanza concludes:

> For liftin' hearts an' killin' care
> > Music's the charm!

This, in itself, is proof enough of the store Charles set by music. There is evidence that he was a piper too. His conviction of the bagpipes' consoling, curative or inspirational power is manifest in the ingeniously rhymed *Lat's Hear the Pipes*. On his travels through southern Africa in 1891 he even made room among his baggage for pipes which met, alas, a crushing end. At some point, however, the casualty was replaced, for a set featured in the inheritance Charles left his son.

During those early years in Aberdeen, Charles Murray became increasingly drawn towards the Walkers – George, Maggie, Andrew, Mary, Nellie and their mother and father. In letters of condolence written in 1937 and 1940 on the occasion of Walker family bereavements, Charles recalls his indebtedness to them: 'It is 60 years next month (January, 1941) since I went, a boy of 16 to Aberdeen and yours was the first house I visited and yours the first family I knew and you can't think how much it meant to the country loon... it would have been a dreary time if it had not been for all your kindness from that first night when I broke the chair!... You might be surprised to know how many happy memories crowd round me tonight... I have such a clear memory of my last evening with you all when I was leaving for South Africa. I would like you... to know how grateful I have always been to you all. Your hospitality and kindness meant so much and I can never forget it.'

This early friendship was to lead to an enduring alliance between the Murray and Walker families. A graduate of Aberdeen and Edinburgh Universities and some three years younger than Charles, George Walker Smith Walker, son of Alex Walker, a tobacconist in Aberdeen, was a solicitor, later a partner in the firm of Adam, Thomson and Ross, Advocates, Aberdeen. His wife, Isabella (Bella), was daughter of George Jamieson, a grocer in the city. George and Bella had three children: a daughter, Isobel, and two sons, Alex and Douglas. The latter boy has a part to play in the unfolding story. Once Charles had embarked upon his life's work overseas and upon the demands of parenthood, he placed himself under growing obligation to the Walkers for the management of his business affairs and parental responsibilities. This, however, was still some way ahead.

On 9 January 1886, on the expiry of the five-year bond, Charles Murray's apprenticeship with Messrs Walker and Beattie would have concluded. It is a measure of his mentors' satisfaction with his competence and character that they retained him as a "salaried assistant" for a further 18 months. In August 1887, however, he left to take up a position, secured for him by his previous employers, in the Surveyors'

Department of Aberdeen advocates, Davidson and Garden, 7 Union Terrace, and there he worked until his departure in December 1888: destination – South Africa.

Charles Murray and his sister Sarah, Aberdeen, (c. 1887)
James Ewing, Aberdeen

Portrait in oils of Charles Murray, painted by his sister Sarah, 1887
Courtesy City of Aberdeen Art Gallery & Museums Collections
© Estate of Sarah Reid

CHAPTER 3

To South Africa

'Hot youth ever is a ranger,
New scenes ever its desire;'
Hamewith

What was it that prompted the 24-year-old Charles to turn his back on promising prospects, on family and friends, and – possibly least explicably of all – on his beloved Howe of Alford, Donside and Bennachie, and put all to the hazard in a land unknown?

There is perhaps no straightforward answer to the question why the young civil engineer left Scotland. He may have had a whole raft of reasons for seeking employment abroad. Why did he opt for South Africa? According to his own admission, he had at one point had Australia in his sights. Was it to satisfy a yearning for adventure in surroundings altogether different from the sometimes dour North-east? Was it in the hope of making his fortune from the veins of Transvaal gold, lately discovered and even then drawing prospectors in their thousands from Europe? Certainly his training would have equipped him for such work. The reference furnished by his erstwhile employers, Messrs Walker and Beattie, on the eve of his departure for South Africa specifically refers to his suitability for overseas service: "… in every way we have confidence in recommending him, especially for a colonial appointment… "

Had word reached him from a relative, from friends, former colleagues or fellow-countrymen, already in South Africa – and of these there was an abundance – that there were openings there for the skilled and the enterprising? Had he, perhaps, been offered immediate employment or did the suspect state of his health contribute to his decision to emigrate? As far back as 1845, missionary-explorer David Livingstone had remarked upon the infrequency of pulmonary and other diseases in the dry, invigorating climate of the *veld*.

Some at home there would have been who deplored "the folly of a nice laddie giving up a steady job at a pound a week" for the uncertainty of foreign parts. The impact of his decision on his family can only be imagined. So far as his sister was concerned, he himself admits that he did not always see eye to eye with her. She might, therefore, have bidden him "Farewell" with equanimity. Moreover, since southern Africa was subsequently to be her home too, she could have found herself in sympathy with his motives.

The parting of father and only surviving son cannot have been easy. Both Peter Murray and Charles, however, were resilient, undemonstrative, extrovert; men of manifold interests and talents. Their busy days would have left no time for brooding. Being a devout parish-church man (although the same cannot be said of his son), Peter had the assurance of his faith that, wherever Charles went, whatever dangers he confronted, never would he be beyond Divine care. With hindsight, by way of consolation to the Murray family, the point might be made: no emigration, no poetic creation. Many families, Scots among them, "lost" children to the colonies at this period. Perhaps, however, the "Empire" was viewed not as exile but as an extension of the motherland.

As the year 1888 drew towards its close, Charles – a tall, lean, fresh-faced, alert young man, judging from an 1887 portrait executed by his sister, Sarah – was finalising preparations for departure. In his luggage he made room for at least one substantial volume of Scots verse, William Walker's lately-published 673-page, critical anthology, *Bards of Bon-Accord 1375-1860*. This was to be a constant companion, finding lodging even on his office shelves once he was established in South Africa. Also among his papers were letters of introduction to contacts abroad who could help him ease into his new surroundings.

On Saturday, 15 December 1888, his odyssey began. Late that evening he made his way to Waterloo Quay, to the wharf of the Aberdeen Steam Navigation Company where the 940-ton, coal-burning, cargo-passenger vessel, the *SS Ban-righ*, Captain Alex Turriff in command, was loading for the regular, twice-weekly, Aberdeen-London run.

No sooner had the voyager embarked than he turned in. Hardly surprisingly, in multi-berth accommodation, sleep was slow in over-taking him. Interest in his fellow-passengers kept him wakeful too. He had come prepared with exercise book and pen to record his impressions and experiences. His observant eye for his travelling-companions and his readiness to listen to and encourage their yarns are at once apparent.

Among those sharing quarters with him were 'two soldiers...

throwing Shakespearian quotations at each other from opposite ends of the cabin; a cockney sailor… struggling into a clean shirt… quite a rare occurrence with him. He was very dirty, extremely short-sighted and the back of his head was as straight up and down as a door… Next to him lay an Emigrant on his way to Dunedin. His most striking peculiarity was the vigorous way in which he slept.'

One passenger in particular awoke Charles's sympathies. 'We had another Emigrant. He came from Ellon and was going to join a brother in Sydney. He was very ill all the way (to London) and took an occasional inspection of some black *nowt*[1] on board to keep up his heart. Last but not least important in our cabin was a baker from Turriff, an unshaven *breet*[2] with the *orra-ist*[3] hat on board.'

The voyage began propitiously, but next night the ship was enveloped in fog and they lay off Gravesend for 48 hours. 'It was dismal – nothing to be seen, and nothing to be heard but bells, bells, ships' bells, barge bells, boat bells, rattling and ringing all round us.'

To while the time away, the shipmates entertained themselves with songs, dramatic recitations and tall tales, such as the following, related by the Turriff baker. He had been travelling steerage on a ship of the Anchor Line. So crowded were they below-decks that at meal-times the steward could not serve them conventionally. Nothing if not enterprising, he cut chunks of beef from the joint and flung one to each man over the heads of the others. They then put a lick of mustard on the only place available – the sleeves of their jackets! On Thursdays – "duff days" – fatalities often resulted from the scramble of those plunging out of their bunks to secure a share of the treat.

Thanks to the fog, the *Ban-righ*, scheduled to dock on Monday, did not come alongside at Limehouse Quay, London, until Wednesday, 19 December. Charles immediately despatched his luggage to the Castle Mail Packets Company wharf, only to learn that his ship, the 380-foot Glasgow-built *Hawarden Castle*, a screw-driven steam vessel, registered tonnage 4380, had just gone. There was nothing for it but to consign his baggage by rail from Paddington Station to catch up with the ship when she put in at Dartmouth, a considerable and unlooked-for expense. Then he telegraphed home.

---

[1] cattle   [2] brute   [3] most disreputable

Charles had connections in London and some errands to undertake. He visited a Mr Preston, spent the night at Wandsworth, leaving with a box of plum-pudding and mince-pies for the voyage – it was Christmas week after all – and collected an aneroid barometer from a Revd. Alfred Philip for delivery to the latter's brother. A visit to the British Museum greatly impressed him, especially viewing Cleopatra's mummy. He had time to take in 'a splendid Punch and Judy show' before rounding off the evening at the Empire Music Hall where he watched 'a good ballet and some middling knock-about business.' With this snatch of London life Charles had to be content.

On Friday, 21 December, he boarded a special train at Paddington for the five-hour run to Dartmouth, stopping briefly at Bath, Bristol and Exeter. Like him, all his fellow-passengers were joining the *Hawarden Castle*. If the landscape *en route* struck him as 'rather monotonous, flat country,' he 'found Dartmouth a most lovely place, green hills studded with quaint houses (that) rise from both sides of the harbour.'

Hawarden Castle, on which Charles Murray travelled to South Africa
(1888–89)

Courtesy World Ship Society

Even after all the passengers had embarked, however, the ship's departure was delayed until 4 am the following day by a strong gale affording the voyage 'quite a rough start' that developed into 'a right good storm in the Bay of Biscay.' In the three-berth cabin with Charles were Mr Cairncross, a young Cape Towner with some command of Dutch, and a Dutchman, Mr Moberus, whose English was limited.

Late on Christmas Eve they entered the Tagus estuary where they had to await the pilot. 'A comic-looking old Pontius he was,' observes Charles. Not until Christmas Day were they able to go ashore at Lisbon. Boarding a tram-car which left from the quay, Charles and an unnamed companion were amused by the conductor, a whimsical fellow who 'laughed heartily at our jokes, and we did the same for his, a considerate proceeding on both sides as neither understood a word the other said.'

Their tram-car took them to the outskirts of the capital. Alighting, they wandered through vineyards and orchards, attaining a slight eminence which gave them a panoramic view. 'Very pretty,' comments Charles, 'but a little spoiled by the scattered houses which gave something of a Cults look. We returned to town by back ways and passed through the older and poorer portions, getting some delightful glimpses of Portuguese life. Tradesmen of all kinds at work sitting on the floor generally, or taking a rest and a tune on a banjo-looking business called a "mandoline". Although we looked about as much as possible, the only good looking female we saw was a servant *deem*[1] shaking mats over a balcony; even then the thought arose that distance helped her charms.'

Before the close of Christmas Day, they were back on board and the *Hawarden Castle* had slipped her moorings and was easing down river for the open waters of the Atlantic. Now established in his temporary home, Charles had an opportunity to observe his fellow-passengers. 'By this time,' he notes, 'we began to… see how much of a miniature world our ship was.' If he was hoping for a romance afloat, he was quickly disillusioned. 'The only eligible young woman aboard, a silly, simpering creature, without a single idea in her head, has made a conquest of the Purser, and – a thorough woman – has managed to set two of the deck officers by the ears.'

The voyage passed agreeably. On 27 December they anchored off Madeira, latitude 32.44N. Then it was that he and his companions began

[1] girl

35

to realise that they were nearing the tropics. So enchanting was the air, 'You caught yourself repeating "balmy" ever so often,' recorded Charles. Visibility was perfect as they steamed south, past Tenerife, the 'weather delightful, never too warm; indeed the whole voyage was the coolest there had been.'

Presently they drew level with Cape Verde, the last land to be sighted until they put in at Cape Town. Before that landfall, they had the landmark of Hogmanay when 'the Scotch *(sic)* passengers, numbering about ten in the 2nd class Saloon, began to move about getting up a concert… By 12 o'clock things got decidedly lively. The Scotch contingent roamed all over the ship first-footing, singing and dancing. The Engineers were Scotch,' he adds, 'so was the Carpenter.'

Charles had looked forward to negotiating the equator. It was with a sense of anticlimax, therefore, that he reported: 'We crossed the line at night so that, being asleep, I cannot say whether we went over it or got it lifted sufficiently to get thro' below.'

The remainder of the voyage passed uneventfully. No date is given for the arrival at Cape Town of the *Hawarden Castle*, but Friday 11 January 1889, seems probable: three weeks to run some 6500 miles is not unreasonable.

Charles had a very clear plan of action. Disembarking as quickly as possible, he made his way 'to Philip Brothers' place in Town' where he was able to have his baggage stowed. Untrammelled then, he did a little exploring until his contact, a Mr Yeoman, was at liberty to take him home for dinner. He next called on two families of Philips, one of whom put him up for the night.

'The Philips were exceedingly kind,' chronicles Charles, 'and on Saturday took me for a drive' – presumably by carriage – 'through Wynberg (to the east) and Constantia (south of Table Mountain), a great wine-growing district, a lively country, queer old Dutch houses and fine avenues of trees – blue gum, oak, etc. I felt quite sorry to leave Cape Town which I did that night.'

The next leg was a 650-mile rail journey to Kimberley, a run he termed 'very pleasant', despite the scorching heat as they headed northeast across the Great Karoo, the arid tablelands where the approach gradients were as much as 1 in 40, forcing the train to a crawl. Arriving at Kimberley – "diamond-town" – on the forenoon of Monday, 14 January, Charles fortunately found a bed at the *Transvaal Hotel*, but was dismayed to learn that no inside-seat would be available on the Johannesburg mail-coach for a fortnight. He turned down an invitation from Dutch travelling companions to share the mule waggon they had hired, preferring an outside-seat on the mail in five days' time for the 300-mile drive. If speed was a concern, he had made the right choice for he reached Johannesburg a week ahead of the muleteers.

During his enforced delay, he was able to form some impression of Kimberley, which stands on the Cape side of the border with the Orange Free State: 'quite a large place but frightfully hot and not very healthy. Altogether I would not care to stay there.' His contact in the town was a Mr Stewart, employed in De Beers Mine. 'He was very pleased to see anyone from Cults and took me over the above-ground workings. The diamonds are found amongst "blue ground". This ground is very hard when brought to the surface; so it is spread out in the open air on what they call the "floors" and soaked with water. It soon gets soft and is then broken up and searched. The black workers all live on the premises in a building called "the compound". They do not get out for months at a time and when they are allowed, they are searched in the most minute manner. In spite of all the precautions taken and the severe penalties for buying diamonds from a Kaffir, a great many diamonds are still stolen. Some of the richest men in Kimberley were what is termed "I.D.Bs"; that is, Illicit Diamond Buyers. Illegal trading in diamonds could result in 20 years or so as a convict on the Cape Breakwater.'

Word of Charles Murray's intended emigration to South Africa would have spread among his acquaintances at home. Those aware of the move would have included some with a South African connection. They might well have seized the opportunity to have the traveller take greetings or gifts on their behalf. It is quite likely, too, that Charles was carrying letters of introduction to smooth his way into employment in the country of his adoption. At any rate his continuing narrative can bear that interpretation.

'I delivered all my letters and saw the people I wanted to and was very glad to get off on Saturday. We had nine passengers, a heavy mail, two drivers and a team of 12 horses. One driver does nothing but work a long whip and he holds no sinecure; it is a case of wallop without stop or break. The drivers are changed every two or three stages, the horses nearly every hour. Altogether we used 324 horses, never having less than 10 at a time. We went right on day and night. During the day the heat was blistering and at night the cold was intense.

'We passed through some pretty country and crossed the Vaal River in a ferry. The roads were in a bad state from late rains; the ruts were sometimes about two feet deep. It was no joke being jolted for 300 miles over roads like these. I do not know whether we felt more surprised or glad when we arrived in Johannesburg without accident. One of our inside passengers,' he notes, 'was a brother of Rider Haggard's.'

How Charles Murray would have completed his journey from Kimberley to Johannesburg, 1889

(From *The Golden Transvaal*)

CHAPTER 4

Prospects and Prospecting

'I've faced the fremt, its strain an' toil, in market an' in mine'
The Alien

The South Africa upon which Charles Murray had set foot was in a state of uneasy peace, but in Johannesburg he was at the flash-point of the impending explosion. To trace the origin of the Anglo-Boer conflict, it is necessary to return to the Cape which, in the mid-17th century, had served as a supply base for Dutch traders *en route* to and from the East Indies. It then became a gateway for land-hungry Boers, anxious to follow their occupations and their faith without harassment.

Other settlers – French, German, British, Portuguese – introduced into Southern Africa the colonial rivalry of European powers. The indigenous population were held as of no account.

Driven from the Cape by the incomers, the Boers sought sanctuary in Natal, in Transorangia, in the Transvaal. Where the Boers went, the British followed, claiming these territories as their own. Little wonder if Boer resentment boiled over in 1880 in what was termed the First Boer War or the First War of Independence. Conventional British tactics proved no match for the swift forays of the Boers. Following the battle of Majuba on 27 February 1881, Britain was only too ready to engage in peace talks. The Transvaal South African Republic was granted a measure of independence.

With the discovery in 1886 of the world's richest veins of gold in the Witwatersrand, the Transvaal leapt into the headlines. Britain's imperialist designs now acquired commercial impetus. The Rand at once became the Mecca for miners and those catering to their needs. So many *uitlanders* (outsiders) – predominantly British – descended upon the Transvaal that the Boers feared for their own balance of power. Hoping to delay the inevitable, they continued to deny the incomers political representation. This was the very pretext Britain needed to justify intervention.

Hostilities, however, were still some years off. The economic climate

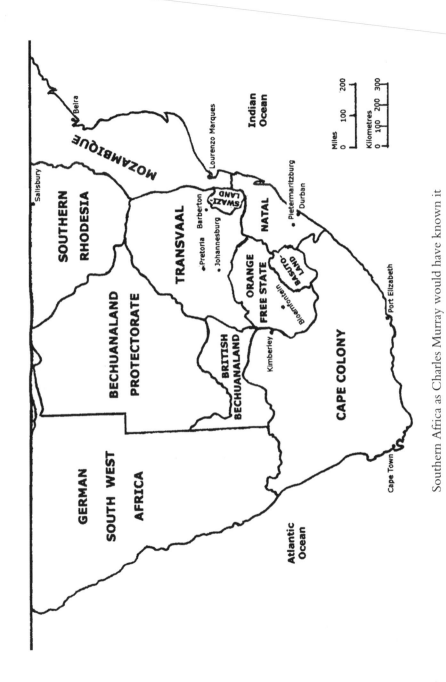

Southern Africa as Charles Murray would have known it

must at that point have favoured business expansion. Charles Murray would, moreover, have prepared the ground ahead of his arrival. Initially, according to the circular of 29 August 1889, submitted in furtherance of his candidature for election to Associate Membership of the Institution of Civil Engineers, " he worked as Assistant to Mr William M Philip, AMICE, Johannesburg," son of the Rev G I Philip of New Deer, Aberdeenshire; but changes were in the offing. Another player was about to come upon the scene.

This was architect Charles Carmichael, newly arrived from UK, a friend of Charles Murray's since at least 1886 through their membership of the Aberdeen Boating Club. It is not improbable that Carmichael, if not indeed both, had made the move to the Transvaal at the invitation of William Philip, for as early as 20 May 1889 the three entered into partnership, establishing the firm of Philip, Carmichael and Murray, Engineers, Surveyors and Architects.

Charles Murray's "Candidate's circular" goes on to list the "principal work" undertaken by him in corporate harness: "an underground survey for the Robinson Gold Mining Company, laying off tramways, erection of houses, and designing and carrying on work of a storage reservoir to contain 25 million gallons, at the same mine. Designing and carrying on work of a storage reservoir for 70 million gallons to supply the 'Princess' and four adjoining gold-mining Companies with water, making surveys of claims, mining properties, etc." And all within eight months of setting foot on the country!

Regrettably, within a year, Carmichael fell ill and on 15 June 1890 died. His place in the partnership was later taken by a man named Leck, who makes no further appearance here.

Even in those opening years, however, not all of Charles Murray's energies were directed towards business. Patiently and covertly he was creating a collection of verse, largely but not exclusively in Scots. One we can date precisely is *Christmas 1890*, conveying greetings to friends or kinsfolk in the North-east of Scotland:

> Altho' sax thousan' mile   Forgettin' new abode
>   O' land and sea,   An' change o' scene –
> Divides us for a while,   Face nor'-nor'-wast an' nod
>   This nicht will we –   To you at Skene.

While hardly poetry, this does demonstrate a rightness of tone, a facility with rhyme, an economy of language and a self-sufficiency that are characteristic of his work.

Early in 1891, impelled partly by a general business decline but also by a sense of adventure, Charles signed on as driver of an ox-wagon bound for Mashonaland – the future Zimbabwe. He was to be one of a party of four – including his cousin Jack – recruited by a London financial firm to replace four prospectors, all of whom had died of fever before they could carry out a mission to peg off gold claims on a concession granted by the Portuguese.

The Square, Johannesburg, 1890s
(From *The Golden Transvaal*)

It should be remembered that this was largely *terra incognita*. The first Pioneers, that is, British soldiers, had entered the territory as recently as 1890. In April 1891, having arranged to rendezvous with the others of his group at Zoutpaisberg, Charles set off from Johannesburg with one wagon – 'a whole tent one,' he explains, 'with springs and a framework (running) from end to end above the boxes for sleeping on.' To pull it he had a total of 26 oxen, but "spanned in" (harnessed) only seven pairs at a time. He admitted he 'had never been in a wagon before and knew nothing about oxen' but pride would not let him back down, especially under the eyes of the accompanying "boys". He paid for his *naïveté* at their first *outspan* (camp): the oxen went missing, delaying their departure until all were rounded up.

Reaching the outskirts of Pretoria late one afternoon, he outspanned close by the Government Hotel. In its backyard, he recalls, stood 'the gallows... a ghastly silhouette against the clear sky.' He spent a day at Pretoria, leaving in the evening by moonlight. Nearly half a century on, he remembered walking ahead of the wagon beyond Wonderboom 'feeling very strange and far from home.' Outside his poems, it was rarely that he voiced yearning for Scotland.

"Far from home" he might be, but that was no barrier to coming across faces familiar from Aberdeen days. Pausing at the Limpopo River, boundary between the Transvaal and Matabeleland, he found that one of two Pioneers on guard at the *drift* (ford) was an acquaintance from the city, while another a little way down-river was a former Aberdeen University student, a football team-mate. Incredibly, at Fort Tuli, a day's trek distant, the soldier managing the Post Office turned out to be an ex-colleague from his office days in Aberdeen.

Sketch of trek-cart by Charles Murray

The journey was not without its lighter moments. Five days out of Fort Tuli, having encamped and had their meal, Charles and his companions astonished their fellow-outspanners by marching in line round their wagon led by a piper, each man following on, making what sounds he could on improvised instruments. Sadly this recital was the last of its kind. Two days later, on a particularly boulder-strewn stretch of track, a jolt pitched the pipes in their box under the wagon wheel, effectively silencing them for good.

In the course of his narrative, Charles seldom makes reference to the indigenous people of the region. In this he was of his age. It went without saying that the (white) colonists saw themselves as superior: natives provided manual labour, but did not otherwise come into the reckoning. On one occasion, however, he recalls that a pretty, lightly-clad, native woman, wife of a chief, ventured too near a group of whites and swiftly retreated when they showed undue familiarity. Like the prophets of old, Charles reflected, 'she had little on her in her own country.'

Despite the hazards of pot-holed roads and having to spend a night bogged down in mid-river, the trekkers made record time to Salisbury, arriving on the morning of 26 June. Salisbury in 1891 consisted of no more than a score of round huts and showed little signs of activity.

Next morning Charles and his team pegged out five "stands", each 60 feet x 100 feet, on what he believed became the city's main street. These they left in charge of an official who sold them at £16 apiece, lodging the proceeds in a Syndicate. Of this transaction they heard no more. Other business, however, now occupied them.

In Salisbury they made contact with a prospector, "Old McWilliam", who waxed enthusiastic over the potential for gold finds in the neighbourhood, showing them some rich stone to back up his claim. He even advised them which areas to concentrate on and which to avoid. It was decided that Charles and one companion, Greenlees, would make for Mazowe – 25 miles north of Salisbury, while Gemmell and Jack Murray would head south-west towards Hartley Hills and Lake Magandis.

Furnished with a sketch-map of the Mazowe road by "Mac" and some papers from the Mining Commission, the party split up to follow their separate fortunes. "Misfortunes" might be a more accurate term. After days of futile "panning", the would-be prospectors returned to rendezvous in Salisbury before trekking off to Umtali, a settlement of 'a few tents and huts' in Manicaland. Crossing into Portuguese territory by 'a very bad road', they left their wagons and exhausted oxen with a driver and went off in further quest of gold. At Umtali they had bought pack donkeys, but the "dry" provisions they were carrying were sodden when the animals fell while negotiating a reed-clogged river. Nor did these exhaust their tribulations. Their camp was burnt out when engulfed in a grass fire and their native carriers, drunk on local beer, deserted.

Disappointed once more in their dream of striking it rich, they deemed it wise to leave the region before the start of the wet-fever season. Over flats teeming with game, including buffalo herds later to succumb to *rinderpest*, they trekked to Mapondas, a Portuguese settlement where they boarded a small river steamer bound for Beira on the Mozambique Channel, facing Madagascar. The steamer, however, grounded on a sand-bank and they completed their voyage in an open boat.

Even at Beira their troubles were by no means at an end. With dwindling resources, they clung to the hope of a south-bound steamer. It was no consolation that they found themselves part of a large and growing muster of destitute miners, deserted by fortune, relying on charity for their next morsel. A concert to raise funds for the distressed was held on 18 November 1891, at which was sung a piece entitled *The Disappointed Prospectors,* words by – Charles Murray. It begins:

> We once were young and stalwart – it's many months ago –
> For lately we've got thinner every day;
> We wander sad and lone, we're reduced to skin and bone,
> And the little hair that's left us now is grey!

and ends with the *Chorus* –

> Our pants are torn and tattered,
> They're shrunk half up the shin,
> At each step our 'ammunitions' give us pain,
> Yet we raise the chorus strong,
> As we 'swag' our way along,
> 'O! Prospecting we will never go again!'

These verses later found their way into a collection of 40 of Charles Murray's earliest poetic endeavours, the short-lived *A Handful of Heather,* printed in 1893 by Lewis Smith & Son, Aberdeen, for private circulation. Many had already appeared in periodicals and their reception may have induced Charles to set aside his diffidence and submit them for scrutiny. They embrace poems in the Doric, recalling the scenes, seasons, situations and personalities of home; and poems in English including the following playful epigram, *Retroussé*, a *salut d'amour*, perhaps addressed to the girl he was to marry:

> A nose tip-tilted may a classic profile mar
> But one gets all the better at the lips;
> Who stops to criticise the handle of the jar,
> Which holds the heavenly nectar that he sips?

No sooner had the slim volume been sent forth, however, than the mistrustful author took fright. He recalled and destroyed all the copies he could retrieve. Fortunately – from the literary historian's standpoint, if not the creator's – at least one copy survived, enabling the enthusiast to assess the writer's developing talent and critical acumen. Of the "handful" of 40 poems, 13 were retained, some with minor modifications, to re-appear in the first edition of his next poetic venture.

Lest it be thought that Charles and his three companions have been altogether abandoned in Mozambique, the narrative resumes with the assurance that after three anxious weeks the patience of the four adventurers was rewarded. They took passage on a vessel which called at Lourenço Marques (modern-day Maputo) before dropping them at Durban on Christmas Day 1891. Having shopped for some clothes to replace the rags they were wearing, they made the 60-mile journey to Pietermaritzburg where they spent the week-end before returning to Johannesburg. They arrived with three shillings amongst the four of them.

In their absence, the economic situation had not improved. After eight months on the road, trekking and camping, Charles had little taste for office life. His business partner, moreover, had married and had spent even the absentee's entitlements. For the next five years, therefore, Charles found employment – and not particularly congenial employment – as Surveyor to the Ferreira, the Wemmer (1894) and the Worcester gold mines on the Rand, and it was as a mine surveyor on a salary of £500 per annum that on 31 July 1895 in Johannesburg he took a wife.

CHAPTER 5

Marriage and Homecoming

"It's time the ane I trysted wi' cam' hame!"
The Maid o' the Mill

Charles Murray's bride was Edith Emma Rogers, third child and eldest of eight daughters in the 13-strong family of businessman, financier and philanthropist, W H Rogers and Jane Rogers (*née* Gusterton).

William Heyward and Henry Adams Rogers were the sons of Devonshire-born John Benjamin Rogers, a Cape Colony settler of about 1840, and his wife, Emma Heyward Bishop, of English parentage but born in Mowbray, South Africa, in 1827. J B Rogers, described as a "writer", died in 1869. His widow, however, lived on until 1897, a dainty, porcelain-fine figure of old-world grace, an enchanting hostess animated by sparkling conversation. In company she would turn to each of her guests, giving her undivided attention. It was hard to realise that she was altogether blind. She lived at Rosebank on the outskirts of Cape Town in an elegantly-appointed thatched cottage, fragrant with lavender and dried roses, the perfect setting for Grandma Rogers to hold court in muslin cap, ringlets bobbing, hands silk-mittened.

It was to their mother that William and Henry owed their entry into the world of business at the Cape. In the early 1870s, however, prompted no doubt by the discovery of fabulous deposits of diamonds at Kimberley, 650 miles to the north east, they left Cape Town and set up a fashion-store in Market Square, old Kimberley, catering for ladies and gentlemen of means. As their backers, they had the well-established firm of Hamilton Ross and Co. They themselves chose to trade as "Rogers and Brother", a name that became synonymous with quality and fair dealing. A contemporary, W B Taylor, recalls those pioneering days 'when the Market Square was invaded by hundreds of wagons and oxen every morning, and the red sanded earth churned up and in rain turned into mud which was ever strong with the scents of ammonia.'

Highly regarded by the digger-community and, on moving to the centre of Kimberley, by the townspeople, "Rogers and Brother" presently took on also the role of booking-office for Gibson Brothers' coaches, coaches that bore to the Rand in their thousands pioneers in quest of gold. In 1884, his civic virtues recognised, William Rogers became a member of Kimberley Town Council and, before long, mayor.

To men of enterprise and courage, the development of the Rand and the growth of Johannesburg must have been irresistible. As soon as opportunity offered, William, acting for a Kimberley Syndicate, moved to the Rand and established commercial relations with the firm of H Eckstein & Co. Appreciating the business acumen of the Rogers brothers, leading companies, such as Alfred Beit and Barnato Brothers, appointed them to their boards. They became directors of land and town companies and served on corporation and water boards.

The volume and variety of work that the Rogers brothers undertook and the dedication they brought to it beggar belief. William, for instance, was one of the founder-members of the Witwatersrand Agricultural

William Heywood Rogers (c. 1900), father-in-law of Charles Murray
(From *The Golden Transvaal*)

Society. Their joint activities ranged from social concerns like hospitals and churches, to industries such as forestry and mining. They witnessed the vast expansion of the gold industry, indeed were involved in its direction. William even donned the mantle of miller, acquiring a share in the Premier Milling Company, incidentally perhaps prompting one of Charles Murray's poems. In all the brothers did, however, service not self prevailed.

William's daughter Edith, the future Mrs Charles Murray, was born at Cape Town on 21 April 1871, but had been sent to Britain to a private establishment at Ealing, kept by a Mrs Hebb, for at least part of her schooling. In her family, however, it was not thought seemly for daughters to equip themselves to earn a living, rather to acquire social graces and accomplishments.

Edith Emma Rogers, Charles Murray's wife-to-be,
aged about 20 (1891)

When and where Edith and Charles first met are matters for conjecture. It must have been prior to 23 May 1892, the date of the celebration held at Doornfontein to mark her parents' Silver Wedding. Edith's copy of the dance-card printed especially for the occasion survives and shows she was partnered at item 15, "Sir Roger de Coverley", by "Pater", the family's possibly jocular term for "father", and at item 8, "Waltz", by "Chs. Murray". Four months later, on 30 September 1892, Charles features as Edith's partner at least six times on the dance-card produced for the "1st Annual Caledonian Ball" at Johannesburg. By the "2nd Annual Caledonian Ball" on 7 September 1893, "C.M." appears no fewer than nine times on Edith's card.

It comes as no surprise that Edith lost her heart to this engaging Scot. Many have remarked upon his striking appearance: tall, lean, athletic, eagle-featured. In personality and character, one sensed that here was someone out of the ordinary. Longer acquaintance would serve only to confirm appreciation of the essential worth of the man, modest, accomplished, shrewd, with a genuine love and understanding of his fellows, non-judgemental, a staunch friend, a trustworthy employee, a just and supportive chief, an entertaining companion with a keen sense of humour and the ability to keep things in proportion. As if these attributes were not enough, there were his poetic gifts. Edith was totally captivated by his love letters. Understandably only the more temperate of these are in the public domain. The others, wrote Edith after her husband's death, these were the true poems.

Charles was no less enamoured of Edith. Taken with her beauty, he came to realise her sterling qualities of character and the wisdom of his choice. During their courtship he was quietly at work, adding to his store of verse. It is at least arguable that two or three, perhaps more, of his poems were inspired by Edith. A case could be made for *The Witch o' the Golden Hair, In the Gloamin'* and particularly for *The Maid o' the Mill*. The last begins:

> The cushie doos are cooin' in the birk,
>   The pee-weets are cryin' on the lea,
> The starlings in the belfry o' the kirk
>   Are layin' plans as merry as can be.
> The mavis in the plantin' has a mate,
>   The blackbird is busy wi' his nest,

Then why until the summer should we wait
When spring could see us happy as the rest?

And concludes:

"There are ower mony maidens at the Mill,
It's time the ane I trysted wi' cam' hame!"

Edith, as has been noted, was one of eight daughters in a family associated with milling and on 31 July 1895 Charles's wish was fulfilled: "… the ane (he) trysted wi' cam' hame!" Next day, the following account appeared in a local South African newspaper:

Charles Murray, studio portrait, South Africa 1894

51

MURRAY – ROGERS

One of the smartest weddings we have had for a long time took place at St Mary's yesterday afternoon, in the presence of a large and fashionable assemblage, the bridegroom being Mr Chas. Murray and the bride Miss Edith Rogers... The bride wore a Worth-like confection of ivory silk with train of rich brocade, and a prettily arranged tulle veil. She also carried a handsome flower bouquet. Four of the bride's sisters acted as bridesmaids, the two elder ones being charmingly attired in cream *crépons* with touches of rose pink velvet and hats to match, while the two little ones looked perfect pictures in cream Empire frocks with quaint bonnets lined with pink... Mrs Rogers' stylish gown of flowered silk with smart little bonnet deserves special mention. A reception followed the ceremony, at the residence of the bride's parents, Mr and Mrs W H Rogers, and there the happy pair were toasted and congratulated by a host of friends prior to their departure on their wedding trip. The wedding presents were numerous and valuable. In honour of the occasion a number of Mr Rogers' colleagues on the Sanitary Board attended the wedding, the usual board meeting being postponed in consequence.

Principals and guests at the wedding reception of
Charles and Edith Murray, 31 July 1895

Despite long, enforced separations, their marriage of close on 46 years was characterised by deep attachment, utter fidelity and mutual respect. On more than one occasion, Charles expressed gratitude to his wife for the refining graces she had brought to his uncouth ways.

Charles Murray (right) mine-surveyor, the Transvaal, 1890s

In the mid 1890's, certainly by 1896, Charles had been appointed manager of the New Florida Gold Mining Company and it was at the New Florida, on 5 June 1897, that the Murray's first child, a son – William Dunn – was born. "Dunn" was in tribute to a good friend, J Nicol Dunn, Managing Editor of the *The Scots Observer*, who had been of substantial help to Charles in having his poems published.

Regrettably the New Florida post turned out unsatisfactory and Charles found himself out of work for six months. Not until 1 February 1898, was he again in employment – as manager of the York Gold Mining Company Limited, Johannesburg, at a salary of £1000 per annum. In addition, a sum not exceeding £5 per month was allowed for servants' wages. By this time he held a Mine Inspector's Certificate, granted by the Government. Once more, however, man and job proved mismatched and, as he later wrote, 'to my great content I got the sack and went on my first trip home.'

Not everyone was "content" at his departure. Feelings were mixed at the West Rand Caledonian Society, for the members were bidding at least a temporary farewell to their Chief and a founding father, to boot. *The Krugersdorp Standard* of Saturday, 19 August 1899, reports in whimsical style the gathering of 'all the good Scotties... to drink whusky *(sic)* and sing songs and things.' In token of their appreciation, members presented Charles with an elaborate and finely executed illuminated address, to which a verbal description does scant justice. Within a border of thistles, a piper is depicted in the lower left corner, in the lower right a male highland dancer and between them a reclining female figure holding a pick against a mineworks background. The scroll reads in part:

> The continued success of our Society, in the foundation of which you took a most prominent part, is undoubtedly due, not only to your unflagging zeal and indomitable energy, but also to the tact with which you have guided it through its infancy and the good fellowship which you have, by personal example, stirred up in the hearts of the members.

The address concludes with wishes for "an enjoyable holiday" and hopes of soon welcoming back the Chief and his wife "to the Country in which you have so many friends." To Mrs Murray they gave "a handsome diamond necklace."

Charles had no lack of inducements to visit Scotland. Besides the longing to see his father again after an absence of more than ten years, to tread familiar ways once more and gaze at cherished landscapes, there was the pride in introducing to Donside kinsfolk his wife (now pregnant with their second child) and two-year-old Billy, the first Murray grandchild. Then there was the growing likelihood of war in southern Africa between Boer and later incomer that could endanger his family and inevitably disrupt industry, not least gold-mining in the Transvaal. As a further spur, there was the prospect, downplay it as he might, of seeing through to publication a fresh collection of verse – 34 poems he had gradually been accumulating and meticulously refining. These, he had been persuaded, warranted public exposure, for at least two-thirds of them had already found a welcome in the pages of periodicals. The collection was to constitute the first edition of *Hamewith*, the title forever associated with Charles Murray.

These were all entirely laudable incentives for heading home. What was totally absent was any thought of personal safety, of flight from involvement in impending hostilities. On the contrary, the Boer War was only 12 days old when Charles, writing from *Upperhaugh* – his father's house near Alford – to the War Office, London, volunteered to serve. The response was swift and, to Charles, devastating. Acknowledging receipt of his letter of 23 October 1899, it expressed "regret that no opportunity presents itself of utilising your services as you desire in South Africa." It was signed by the Assistant Adjutant General, Royal Engineers. Charles had evidently hoped that his professional qualifications would open doors. No doubt he had also referred to his previous six-year enlistment in the 1st Aberdeenshire Royal Engineers (Volunteers).

Bitterly disappointed as he was at this setback, Charles was not deterred. Ten weeks after the safe delivery in Aberdeen, on 26 January 1900, of his daughter, Edythe Margaret, he took ship for South Africa, reportedly travelling steerage of necessity, and 'leaving the family behind with no money,' as he later, much later, admitted in a letter to his younger daughter. We can only imagine the conflict of duties, real and perceived, he had to resolve before reaching this harsh decision.

Some light on what prompted such a resolution of his dilemma is shed in another letter addressed by Charles from 24 Desswood Place, Aberdeen, on 30 March 1900. It was primarily a letter of condolence to

Anthony McCreadie, his former school-master, who had written to inform him of the death on 14 December 1899, of his wife, Margaret, herself it will be recalled also a Gallowhill School teacher, and fondly remembered by Charles. The latter promises to call on his old teacher when paying a final visit to Alford before leaving for South Africa on 7 April, explaining: 'I have felt all along I ought to be out doing something for the cause in which so many of my friends have given up their lives… '

From this same letter we learn, too, that *Hamewith* is on the threshold of publication. 'I have a small volume of Scots verse in the press,' Charles writes, 'and I hope to send you a copy before I go. I hope you will care to have it as the work of an old pupil even should you find no merit in it otherwise. When I first thought of publishing, I looked forward to the pleasure of sending a copy to Mrs McCreadie and I am sure on that account you will be glad to have it.'

Interestingly enough it was to Mrs McCreadie that Charles had sent, in his apprentice years, a piece of juvenile verse celebrating his nascent moustache. All that survives, if more there was, is the couplet:

It's comin' noo,
Abeen my mou'.

CHAPTER 6

The First *Hamewith*

'A small volume of Scots verse'
Letter to Anthony McCreadie 30 March 1900

Charles entrusted publication of what was to be the first edition of *Hamewith* to Messrs D Wyllie & Son, Aberdeen. Between mid-blue board covers, bearing in gilt lettering the title – split between two lines so that *HAME* appeared above *WITH* – and the monogram 'C' embracing 'M', were contained 34 poems carefully selected and meticulously revised. A frontispiece, depicting a scene from the work entitled *A Green Yule*, had been furnished by the versatile Aberdeen artist Robert Douglas Strachan whose talents embraced the creation of such diverse forms as political cartoons and stained glass windows, the latter including commissions for King's College and St Machar's Cathedral, Aberdeen.

Indications are that he and Charles were friends rather than simply artist and patron, for Strachan attended a complimentary dinner for the returned exile in 1900 and subsequently executed several pieces, among them: a book-plate in 1902; two portraits of Charles – one in charcoal (1900), the other in oils (1906); and a further illustration for the second edition of *Hamewith* (1909). In 1901, moreover, he sought a favour from Charles: namely, assistance in finding a post in South Africa for a young man by the name of Charles Christie who was to make his own contribution to the story of Charles Murray. Whether the latter raised a finger to smooth the younger man's entry into the Transvaal Public Service will never be known, but his appointment in July 1902 was for Charles Christie the start of long-term employment in the Public Works Department where he served under Charles Murray and, like so many, came to admire him unreservedly.

Of the poems comprising *Hamewith*, thirteen had been salvaged and critically reviewed following their publication in the privately printed *A Handful of Heather* (1893). Ten of the thirteen had first appeared in various periodicals and, of these, two – *Winter* and *Spring in the Howe o' Alford* – had been expanded.

"THIS·IS·THE·ONLY·FAULD" A GREEN YULE.

Frontispiece by R Douglas Strachan, appearing in the 1900 and
1909 editions of *Hamewith*
Courtesy Mrs Una D Wallace

For close on eleven years Charles had been absent from Scotland. Many and many a time, however, he must have re-visited his home country in imagination, so graphically are his word-pictures drawn. Scenes, seasons and situations are evoked; characters come to life; tales of bravado, treachery, sadness stir the reader; reflections sardonic, sombre, whimsical invite sympathy or delight; "occasional" pieces pay homage to two fellow-poets – Robert Louis Stevenson and Burns. All this is grist to his mill. Territorially Charles may limit himself to North-east Scotland, but in topics and treatment he is prepared to be venturesome.

Witness, for instance, his evocation of Hell's gate that opens *The Deil an' the Deevilock*:

> The muckle Deil lay at the mirk pit mou',
>> An' hard at his heel lay a Deevilock;
> While the brimstane reek wi' an upward spew
>> Swirled roon' baith the Deil an' the Deevilock.

Then, from *A Green Yule* there is this cameo of a "draggled hoodie craw" restlessly surveying a graveyard in eager anticipation of an approaching *cortège*:

> Sae up an' doon the tablin' wi' a gloatin' roupy hoast,
>> He haps, wi' twistit neck an' greedy e'e,
> As if some deil rejoicin' that anither sowl was lost
>> An' waitin' for his share o' the dregie.

Contrast is a device frequently employed by Charles, as in the opening stanzas of *Winter*:

> Now Winter rides wi' angry skirl
> On sleety winds that rive an' whirl,
> An' gaberlunzie-like plays tirl
>> At sneck an' lozen.
> The bairns can barely bide the dirl
>> O' feet gane dozin.

The ingle's heaped wi' bleezin' peats
An' bits o' splutt'rin' firry reets
Which shortly thow the ploughmen's beets;
                 An' peels appear
That trickle oot aneth their seats
                   A' ower the fleer.

The Lettergae, consisting of two longish stanzas, again demonstrates contrast. Verse one opens:

On Sundays see his saintly look –
    What grace he maun be feelin',
When stridin' slawly ben the pass,
    Or to the lettrin speelin'!

Week-days are different, as verse two reveals:

But see him now, some workin' day
    When aproned in his smiddy,
An' mark the thuds 'at shape the shoon,
    An' dint the very studdy;

In *The Miller Explains* the humour, an element in many of the poems in this collection, is broader but not astringent. It rarely was. Charles looked at human failings with a tolerant eye, aware of our common frailty. The miller defends his liking for drink:

Week in an' week oot, when I'm millin',
    The sids seem to stick in my throat;
Nae wonder at markets I'm willin'
    To spend wi' a crony a groat.
An' if I've a shaltie to niffer,
    Or't may be some barley to sell,
An oonslockened bargain's aye stiffer –
    Ye ken that fu' brawly yersel'.

Happily married himself, Charles could nevertheless feel sympathy for hen-pecked husbands, such as the eponymous Jeames, followed all too swiftly to the grave by his shrewish wife:

> It seem'd richt unco – faith, 'twas hardly fair,
> Just when he thocht to slip awa' at last
> An' drap for aye the trams o' wardly care –
> The muckle gates aboon were barely fast
> Ere she was pechin' up the gowden stair,
> An' fleechin' Peter till he let her past.

The miller too, ambushed by his wife on his unsteady way home from a night out with his cronies, had likewise to suffer her barbed recriminations:

> She bann'd the moulter an' the mill,
> The intak, lade, an' dam,
> The reekit dryster in the kil',
> Syne back again to Tam.
> Till dark – the minister himsel'
> I'll swear he couldna stap her –
> Her teethless mou' was like a bell,
> Her tongue the clangin' clapper.

Sometimes the humour is tinged with irony, as in *"My Lord"*:

> Nakit tho' we're born an' equal,
> Lucky anes are made Police;
> An' if civil life's the sequel,
> Honours but wi' age increase,
> Till a Baillie, syne selected
> Ruler ower the Council Board,
> An' tho' never re-elected,
> "Ance a Provost, aye 'My Lord.'"

The irony may in some instances be directed at the poet himself, challenged in *The Remonstrance* for time misspent upon "worthless" versifying:

Noo man, hoo can ye think it richt
To waste your time, nicht after nicht,
An' hunker in the failin' licht
      Wi' moody broo,
Like some puir dwinin' thewless wicht
      Wi' death in view?

The poet responds with characteristic modesty:

Tho' loud the mavis whistles now
An' blackbirds pipe fae ilka bough
An' laverocks set the heart alowe –
      Mid a' the plenty
You'd miss upon the wayside cowe
      The twitt'rin' lintie.

★   ★   ★   ★   ★

Nae care hae I, nor wish to speel
Parnassus' knowe, for mony a chiel
Has tint his time, his life as weel,
      To claim a bit o't:
I only crave a wee bit biel'
      Near han' the fit o't.

"*Bydand*" and *The Outlaw's Lass* are ballads of love betrayed. *The Witch o' the Golden Hair* is a hymn to the beloved, an inventory of her charms, each acquired from an external source – with one exception:

The dimples three that you still can see
    Are a' she can claim her ain,
For in Nature fair naught can compare
    Wi' them; they are hers alane.

The vein of whimsy that contributes to the appeal of *The Witch* runs through another delightful piece – *In the Gloamin'*. One of a pair of lovers complains that all nature is conspiring to deny them the privacy courtship craves:

The mavis told his mate to hush
    An' hearken fae the tree;
The robin keekit fae a bush
    Fu' pawkily an slee.
An' now they sing o' what they saw
    Whenever we gang roamin';
They pipe the very words an' a'
    We whispered in the gloamin'.

The speaker finds consolation in the hope that winter or a despoiled hive may end the intrusions, while (his) thoughts will continue to dwell upon (his) sweetheart.

In contrast to these delicate love poems is *Virgil in Scots*, the gory tale of the blinding of Cyclops at the hands of Ulysses' men, a vigorous muscular paraphrase from Book III of the *Aeneid*.

I saw him, sirs, as sure's I live,
    Ance as he lay at easedom,
Twa buirdly chiels tak' in his neive,
    Syne careless fac him heeze them.
They fell wi' sic a dreadfu' thud,
    Whaur stanes lay roon' in cairns;
The causey ran wi' thickened blood
    Like stoorum made wi' harns.

To the quiet surprise of the unassuming author, *Hamewith* proved an immediate and enduring success. It met with critical acclaim, but more significantly it was acknowledged by his fellow-countrymen, especially those of the North-east, as a recognisable voice recreating familiar scenes, seasons, situations and personalities, from *Spring in the Howe* to *The Hint o' Hairst*, from *The Maid o' the Mill* to *The Antiquary*. A new *makar* had made his entrance. His sadly all too infrequent re-appearances in print confirmed among his admirers that there had emerged a maturing talent manifesting growing mastery of his art: greater economy and precision of language; deepening insight into character and circumstance; a readiness to experiment in rhyme-scheme and metre.

These creative gifts and his adventurous spirit led Charles Murray at some unspecified but early dates to try his hand at prose. There survive

This sketch of Charles Murray by his friend R Douglas Strachan enhanced
the menu at a complimentary dinner for the exile home on leave in 1900.
Courtesy Mrs Una D Wallace and the Trustees of the National Library of Scotland

manuscripts of an unfinished play and three short stories, one untitled and incomplete. The play, a comedy in the Doric initially entitled *The Dominie has visitors* but subsequently re-named soberly *Education,* demonstrates that the author appreciates that conflict lies at the heart of drama. He presents a range of entertaining characters caught up in an intriguing plot and engaging in rich and fluent dialogue.

The first of the short stories, *A Modern Joseph,* tells of a church minister who has a dream. It is interpreted by a released jailbird, the "modern Joseph", whose fine for poaching the minister has paid. The interpretation persuades the latter to renounce his conceited ways. Although lacking the humour associated with Charles Murray, the plot is original and imaginative.

Appearing under the pseudonym "Robbie Elrick", the second tale, *The Dambrod,* concerns a church elder who plays draughts with the devil – and wins. Again the situation is fancifully conceived and a degree of tension is built up.

The third story involves a foundling and begins somewhat lugubriously: "O' the times, the weary weary times". Even with pages missing, it is still over-long. To assess it justly in its partial state is impossible but it seems to lack direction and point. The economy, discipline and precision of poetry, one concludes, better suited the literary abilities of Charles Murray for he never again strayed from his first love.

CHAPTER 7

Matters Military and Civil

'Wᴇ couldna pass the challenge by'
A Sough o' War

Despite the principled motives that wrenched him from his family in April 1900, Charles found on arrival in Cape Town towards the end of the month that it was no easy matter to persuade the British military authorities there to engage him. After lengthy delays, however, his persistence paid off. He was ultimately accepted for service and given joint responsibility for setting up the Railway Pioneer Regiment to which he was assigned with the rank of lieutenant.

Not until 3 December 1900, was he able to write to Edith (still in UK) and convey this news:

'My Dearest Wife,
    You have the honour – an honour I expect you never aspired to or will be particularly delighted over – of being the wife of a commissioned officer (*sic*) in the irregular forces of our great army…
    Our district is to be from the Vaal to Pretoria and Potchefstroom to Standerton; the duties to guard the line, convoys, etc. I am afraid we will not have much chance of seeing our brother Boer.'

Clearly Charles was disappointed not to have been given a combatant role.

His letters to his wife are, as ever, warmly affectionate, full of longing to be re-united with his family:

'Yes, Sweetheart, I will be careful of myself, and you can look forward to coming out to a military-looking hubby with no cough and who never wants to be away from you again.
    'I feel as if I want nobody and nothing but just my own three who are now looking at me from the wall. I feel jealous of every man I see walking with a woman.'

Lieutenant Charles Murray, Railway Pioneer Regiment, the Transvaal,
during the Second Boer War (1900–1902)

Reflecting on the dedication "TO MY WIFE" of the lately published *Hamewith*, he writes to her:

'... it struck me one night how wild I would have been if I had dedicated these verses – uncouth and unworthy as they are – to anyone else than you; not that I ever thought of doing so but that terrible Scots reticence and dislike of any outward show of affection might have prevented me only that, under the sunshine of your love, the naturally bleak and barren soil has blossomed into some approach to cultivation.

'I do not know if you will be pleased or disappointed to know that I feel more like writing love letters than even in our engagement days, those days when I dared not touch you and could not kiss that sweet little bit of white throat however much I wanted to. Sweetheart, I wish you felt like that too, not a kind of accustomed affection "to the daddy" but the old love for your "man".

'... I hope the change (presumably of scene) has done you good, and yet you unkind thing you suggest I ought to have married a Scots girl. I don't like you to say things like that...

'... Stevenson says "To marry is to domesticate the Recording Angel" but the true wife is not the hard unforgiving judge but the kindest and most sympathetic of angels, not one to hide troubles from but to bring them to and, my love, you have been all this and more to me. Perhaps, if you had been harder and more worldly, you might have driven me to more worldly success and you might not be so poor today, but with a wife like that, mere money-making would bring no reward for me, and then in striving to get on, I might have become less particular about the means. ... I am getting into a moralizing mood which I had no thought of when I started to tell my little wife how much I loved her and wanted her.

'I hope our Peggy (Edythe Margaret) will grow up to be like her mother. We will still have to get a dark haired blossom to complete our bouquet but that will have to be an after consideration. Meantime I am jealous of the country that holds you, the people who see and speak to you, even the heather-scented breezes that take liberties with your hair – my hair... '

Word of her husband's commissioning in the irregular British forces in South Africa met with an immediate response from Edith Murray, still languishing in UK. She set about securing an "indulgence passage" for herself and their two children, in hope of an early reunion with Charles – her "Charlie". He, on his part, in a letter full of love and longing, expressed regret that after an eight-month separation she had to contemplate another winter on her own. Indeed, such was the disruption occasioned by war that it was not until 17 September 1901 that, having reached Cape Colony, she was able to inform Charles that her permit to join him in Pretoria had been issued.

By then, however, he was no longer a serving military officer. Without having had the chance of "a crack at brother Boer", as he put it, he had on 1st June of that year resigned his commission to accept the proffered position of Deputy Inspector of Mines, with the Department of Mines, Transvaal. No doubt his varied and increasingly responsible posts in private sector mining and Mine Inspector's certification had led to this invitation and appointment. He had set his foot upon the Public Service ladder.

Promotion followed rapidly. Posted first to Johannesburg, he was presently despatched to Krugersdorp – 'my old District,' he terms it – some 20 miles to the north-west, to open the office of the Engineering Branch of the Mines Department, before being transferred to Pretoria in September with the rank of Acting Inspector to repeat the process. His 'ultimate destination,' he reports was supposedly Barberton, 'A lovely place amongst the mountains but hot as … an out-of-the-way spot being, as country folks used to say, "at the back o' Gweed's elbuck".' His district there was to be 'about the size of Britain.' He admits ruefully, 'I can't say I am enamoured of Civil Service life. There is so much red-tape about I run the risk of hanging myself whiles.'

The war in South Africa was far from over. No aspect of life remained unaffected. Housing was a case in point. With considerable difficulty Charles had rented part-furnished accommodation in Pretoria. On 16 October, with the full knowledge and consent of the Assistant Commissioner of Police and in anticipation of his wife and children joining him shortly, he moved in.

His bachelor existence ended on the evening of 8 November when his family duly arrived from Cape Town. At noon the following day, despite having paid the November rent in advance and having a six-month lease, he was instructed by the Superintendent of Police to move out forthwith. An appeal to the Military Governor fell on deaf ears and the family were under notice to leave before the end of the month. Charles Murray, however, was nothing if not tenacious. He pursued his case right to the top, to Lord Alfred Milner, the High Commissioner for South Africa, no less. According to a letter of 3 December to the Walker family of Aberdeen, Charles was expecting nightly to come home 'to find my piano – which is about all the Boers left us – standing in the street and the family sitting greetin' on the top of it.'

'This is not a very good place for Scots folks,' he continues, 'especially at this season, as there has not been a drop of whisky in the town since St Andrew's Night which was last Saturday. Even the mosquitoes – who only get it second-hand – wear a dejected tee-total sort of a look.'

Apart from housing problems, Charles did not find the work congenial. The following year (1902) saw him transfer to the Crown Titles Office where he became Registrar. This meant a move back to Johannesburg. His role was to assist the Public Works Department in such matters as the conservation of Government-owned, fixed property on city sites; emending flawed titles to property; and investigating suspect transfers of property ownership.

This sounds a very dry, involved, legalistic business, but it was one demanding foresight, clarity of mind, infinite patience, tact extra-ordinary and bulldog tenacity. It was also crucially important, especially in the aftermath of a destructive war that had been brought to a bitter close by the Treaty of Vereeniging as recently as 31 May 1902. The country was impoverished, its infrastructure wrecked, its workforce dispersed, its industries disrupted. It was a matter of starting over again.

An on-the-spot reporter, however, found reason for optimism. Charles Christie, the young Scot who had lately come to South Africa and found employment in the Public Service, Transvaal, said of Johannesburg:

'The town was full of movement and activity. The wheels of the mining industry were slowly revolving. Everybody was busy clearing up and tidying and, in the off moments, getting some communal life going again. Friendships were being renewed every-where after a long severance. There was a big measure of goodwill and co-operation, for much racial friction (i.e. between Boer and Briton) had been dissipated by the war.'

It was well for the future of the Transvaal that the post of Registrar of Crown Titles was held by a man of the calibre of Charles Murray. Possessing an abundance of common sense, determination and integrity, he had also the vision to ensure that prime Government land was held in reserve for major enterprises such as the University of the Witwatersrand and Johannesburg Public Library, not released for baser uses.

The weighty responsibilities of Registrar might have rendered some public servants dogmatic, self-important, unapproachable: not Charles Murray. Again it is to Charles Christie that we owe this vignette of his "Chief" in a work setting.

Towards restoring normality to the Transvaal 'Charles Murray was doing his share, with his pleasant friendliness (and his dyspeptic cough) in a tobacco-scented, poky, dark and homely little room – a place of the happiest memories – in Winchester House. It had in the corner, a miniature fire grate, quite incapable of heating anything, and, for furniture, a trestle table, an uncomfortable chair and a draughtsman's stool. But, in talk with the occupant, nobody noticed the furniture, and comfort had no place in his everyday philosophy.'

The remit of the post of Registrar was later extended to create the Estates Office of the Public Works Department, Charles becoming Estates Officer. His superior, the current Director of Public Works, was Colonel – subsequently Lieutenant-General Sir – George H Fowke, on secondment from the army to assist in establishing the new Civil Service. Although his tenure of this position was brief, he made upon those who served under him, a lasting impression as a man of exceptional mind.

Relations between Charles and his Director were of the most cordial, for both had a large measure of common sense and a genuine concern for their colleagues. Innate ability always awoke in Charles greater admiration than merely acquired knowledge – "what the spoon put in" as the Scots phrase rather disparagingly styles it – and Colonel Fowke possessed a great deal of the former.

In 1905, the Estates Office moved to Pretoria to be incorporated in the Department, with Charles Murray as Under-Secretary for Public Works, Transvaal. This meant, of course, yet another change of address for the Murray family. From Johannesburg they accordingly removed the 37 or so miles north-north-east to the Sunnyside district of Pretoria where they remained – apart from home leave and obligatory (and sometimes lengthy) spells in Cape Town while Parliament was sitting – until 1924, when Charles retired.

'*The Willows*', the Murrays' house, Pretoria

On Colonel Fowke's return to military duty in 1905, he was succeeded as head of the Public Works Department by another military man. This was Captain – later Major-General – R N Harvey, DSO, RE, the former Under-Secretary, whose mantle Charles had now assumed. With him, too, Charles found common ground, sharing as they did a fondness for light topical verse of their own or others' contriving. It was not simply his facility with words, however, that commended Charles to his superiors, but the sheer professionalism and dedication he brought to every task. The greater the responsibility laid upon him, the larger grew his organisational and adminstrative skills. He could look at a problem, reduce it to essentials and provide what he saw as a common-sense solution. Little wonder, therefore, that, when Captain Harvey in his turn moved on in 1906, the post he vacated – Chief Engineer and Secretary, Department of Public Works, Transvaal – went to Charles Murray, initially in an acting capacity, with responsibility also for roads and bridges.

For the Murrays, however, the year 1906 was noteworthy in another

The Murray and Reid families at Yeovil, South Africa (c. 1903).
Standing: Charles Murray (left); Andrew Reid (right) husband of Sarah
Murray. Seated (l. to r.): Billy and Edythe Margaret Murray;
Mollie and Sarah Reid; Edith Murray

regard also: it saw them bound for Scotland on well-earned leave. If previous and subsequent furloughs are any guide, the visit took place towards the end of the year. This presumption is supported by three clues: a painting, a photograph and a letter.

The painting, dated "Xmas 1906", is a three-quarter length study in oils of Charles, in outdoor clothing appropriate for a British winter. To this portrait attaches a story. Apparently, at the sitting, the artist, Murray's friend Douglas Strachan referred to earlier, was having no success in achieving a likeness – not, that is, until his subject rose to leave. Then, hat on head, coat collar turned up against a keen wind, Charles is captured to the life.

Portrait in oils of Charles Murray (1906), the work of R Douglas Strachan
Courtesy Mrs Una D Wallace

The second clue, the photograph, shows three figures standing in a winter landscape, probably within the Haughton Estate, Alford. They represent three generations of the Murray family: grandfather Peter, shotgun in the crook of his right arm; father Charles, similarly equipped; between them, young William, Charles's son, clasping a ferret, the ferret box dangling at the boy's back. A reasonable estimate would put him between 9 and 10 years of age. William having been born in June 1897, the photograph must belong to late 1906, early 1907.

Three generations of Murrays – Peter, young William and Charles

Now the letter: it is one written by Charles from Pretoria on 19 July 1916, to the Reverend James B Duncan, surviving partner of a collaboration with the celebrated collector of folk songs, Gavin Greig. Charles recalls hearing the Reverend Duncan deliver an address on Folk Songs in Alford hall 'On one holiday – is it 4 or 10 years ago?' Reference is made in the letter to a song entitled *Hielan' Hairry* which Charles had alluded to in *The Packman*, a poem first published in book form in the 1909 (London) edition of *Hamewith*. It must, therefore, have been not four but ten years prior to the letter that Charles had attended the Alford lecture. That would place it in 1906, for his next leave was not until 1912.

It is to be hoped that Charles found home leave relaxing and restorative, for a daunting work-load confronted him on his return to South Africa. 'In his new capacity,' (as Chief Engineer and Secretary of Public Works, Transvaal) reported the Johannesburg *Star*, 'he was concerned with the spending of the first million of money distributed by the Public Works Department in a single year; and many of the Government Buildings which are now (1941) among the older features of Johannesburg and the capital, schools all over the Province and the first good roads in it came under his hand.'

CHAPTER 8

Builder in Words; Builder in Stone

'Instead o' vreetin' like a clerk'
The Remonstrance

If the year 1907 had been noteworthy in civil engineering achievement, the year following was memorable on another account. On 7
July 1908 was born the Murray's second daughter, Jean Heather Marris,
the 'dark-haired blossom to complete (their) bouquet,' as Charles had
romantically phrased it. The inclusion of "Marris" in baby Jean's name
was a mark of his regard for classical scholar, W S – later Sir William –
Marris, resident in Pretoria in 1907 and 1908, collaborator with him in
a literary enterprise – translating the poems of Horace into English and
into Scots. In his published anthology, *Odes of Horace in English Verse*, Sir
William thanked Charles for his generous help in "improving" the trans-
lator's verse, "with a grateful memory of many laborious and lively
evenings in Pretoria," terming him *maiore poeta plectro* – the poet with
the greater creative gift. Charles benefited from the other's classical
expertise in late-night sessions at the Willow House, spent in critical
scrutiny and in brushing up his own knowledge of Latin, probably
dormant since Gallowhill days, furnishing the basis for his own accomplished Doric paraphrases of Horace.

Diffident always about making public his "verse", which late in life
he referred to deprecatingly as 'youthful indiscretion', Charles eventu
ally and reluctantly yielded to the urging of enthusiasts to allow a second
edition of *Hamewith* to be canvassed among publishers. Principal among
his persuaders was Charles Christie, his young Scots colleague. Christie
it was who, while on leave in UK in 1908, sought a publisher for the
new *Hamewith* which he believed merited wider exposure than the 1900
one, published in Aberdeen.

His first approaches, however, were rebuffed. It was not until he met
J G Wilson of Messrs Constable that a deal was struck. For all that, Mr
Wilson had stipulations. He required an "Introduction" for the work
and this the novelist John Buchan, a good friend of Charles Murray,

managed to coax from Scottish man of letters, Andrew Lang. A poet himself, Lang pays delicate, if somewhat whimsical, compliment to our author's poetry, terming it "ale (which is excellent)... all brewed from the heather bell... Pure Scots... Mr Murray... is haunted by the scent of peat and bog myrtle, the sound of old words that now are strange... Poetry more truly Scots... is no longer written... "

The publishers, prudent men, insisted too on a guarantee against loss. In accepting that responsibility and undertaking, moreover, to see the book through the press, William Marris no doubt felt he was merely repaying a debt to a friend. Constable's misgivings were unfounded. The success of the 1909 *Hamewith* again far exceeded the expectations of its creator. By 1913 it had reached its ninth impression. Clearly there was a public eager to seize upon this representation of a local landscape, its folk, characteristic flora and fauna, its atmosphere, its cycle of seasons.

The 1909 *Hamewith* contained forty-five poems, eleven of them new, together with *Arles*, retrieved from *A Handful of Heather*. These additions included the paraphrases from Horace and *The Whistle*, a piece first printed in February 1906 in Chambers' Journal and attaining rapid and enduring celebrity. Its deftly-varied, dancing rhythms, its humorous word pictures, its surely-drawn characters, its narrative drive – all ensured it a secure place in the affections of generations of listeners and reciters.

What is striking about this collection is its diversity. Extending the contents did not mean simply more of the same, but an opportunity to touch on new topics and to experiment with form, innovative steps which Charles Murray pursued throughout his creative life. *The Alien*, for example, which had appeared in the *Spectator* of 13 January 1906, stands out from the other poems in being written almost entirely in standard English, doubtless to underscore the estrangement the speaker feels in an environment so unlike his native North-east of Scotland. It is, moreover, one of only a handful of works recounting actual situations experienced by the poet in his life overseas: Charles *had* prospected for gold; he *had* hunted game; he *had* surveyed underground mine workings and known troughs and crests in business. On the other hand, however, *The Alien* shares a feature frequently recurring throughout Murray's poetic output – the use of contrast. A single verse is example enough:

I've faced the fremt, its strain an' toil, in market an' in mine,
    Seen Fortune ebb an' flow between the "Chains,"[1]
Sat late o'er starlit banquets where the danger spiced the wine,
    But bitter are the lees the alien drains;
For all the time the heather blooms on distant Bennachie,
    An' wrapt in peace the sheltered valley lies,
I want to wade through bracken in a glen across the sea –
    I want to see the peat reek rise.

Nostalgia is ever present, if not in the language employed here, certainly in the sentiments. It was in the Doric, however, that Charles felt most at home in verse-making. Not only was it his inherited tongue; it was also the delight of his leisure hours. He was better read in Scots poetry, past and current than most of his contemporaries and put his knowledge to good account in creating his own poems. A case in point is *The Packman*, included in *Hamewith* 1909. The opening lines, the metre and rhyme scheme echo those of an earlier work – Peter McCombie's *Jolly Beggar* with which Charles was familiar, but the latter deals with a sexual encounter while Murray's is a rags-to-riches tale, giving a minutely observed and humorous account of the packman's wares, his sales technique and the roles he successively filled in his rise to prosperity. It is said that Burns laughed aloud as he fashioned *Tam o' Shanter*. The packman likewise leapt to a life of his own, to his creator's huge delight and approbation:

He kent wha got the bledder when the sooter killed his soo,
An' wha it was 'at threw the stane 'at crippled Geordie's coo,
He kent afore the term cam' roon' what flittin's we would see,
An' wha'd be cried on Sunday neist, an' wha would like to be,
He kent wha kissed the sweetie wife the nicht o' Dancie's ball,
An' what ill-trickit nickum catched the troot in Betty's wall,
He was at the feein' market, an' he kent a' wha were fou,
An' he never spoiled a story by consid'rin' gin 'twas true.

---

[1] Barriers outside Johannesburg Stock Exchange creating an enclosure within which brokers, buyers and sellers transacted property and share deals and speculated on gold output.

The 1909 *Hamewith* contained also seven paraphrases in Scots from the works of Horace, the outcome of collaboration between classical scholar William Marris and Charles in the years 1907-08. Horace offers reflections upon life and its uncertainties and upon human relationships. These Charles renders admirably, capturing the spirit and humour of the old poet, but substituting Scottish settings and characters:

> Kirsty, ye besom! auld an' grey,
> > Peer Sandy's wrunkled kimmer,
> Death's at your elbuck, cease to play
> > Baith hame an' furth the limmer.
>
> Ongauns like yours lads weel may fleg
> > Fae lasses a' thegither;
> Tibbie may fling a wanton leg
> > Would ill set you her mither.

Many years later, when his never abundant flow of verses had all but dried up, Charles was prompted by the favourable comments of William Will, a close friend with literary leanings, to resume such paraphrasing. Subsequently he even felt moved to undertake the occasional original piece.

So much for his poetic creativity. His capacity to run the prosaic but crucial and complex Transvaal Public Works Department now deserves attention.

Charles Murray has been described as "a pioneer in the practice of administrative simplification". He deplored disorder and sought to establish procedures to be followed throughout his department. For each type of task a routine was laid down, the simpler the better. Introducing standard designs for schools, hospitals, police-stations, for instances, meant savings of labour, time and money.

Uniformity of approach was matched by standardization of materials and quality control. In brick-making, for example, the benchmark was the "Kirkness brick", devised by an Orkney man, J J Kirkness, at the prompting of Charles. Quality control called for laboratories with test equipment and inspectors qualified to assess the full range of building material. Not only quality, but quantity had to be monitored if departmental funds were to be husbanded. Then precise specifications had to be drawn up to assist not only "in house" but contract tendering.

Thus was built up a climate of trust between the building industry and the Public Works Department whose head was more than content to put work out to tender to the private sector, while the latter welcomed the sounder base for contract letting. Charles also promoted among the principal contractors the creation of an informal association that gave rise to the Master Builders' Federation. This body, together with the Craft Unions, afforded stability to the industry, linking as it did employers, PWD and building trades. Co-operation extended even to sporting fixtures between Federation and Public Works on tennis-court or golf-course and in those Charles naturally participated.

These informal encounters in off-duty hours may have eased negotiations between the parties involved and generated mutual regard. They did not, however, normally lead to any relaxation of the strict business code practised by Charles, not even when devised by feminine wiles. Charles, so the story goes, had reluctantly to decline invitations to dine at the home of a gracious hostess. These engagements, he explained, were costing his Department too dear. One such occasion had elicited a tennis-court. Now an extension to her lawn was her covert aim.

As Registrar of Crown Titles, Charles had had, however, to withstand more serious efforts to secure favours. There were those in the colonial Civil Service of the day who believed themselves entitled to concessions because they had behind them the weight of Lord Milner, former Governor of Cape Colony and currently High Commissioner for South Africa. In that category was Lionel Curtis, who belonged to the coterie of gifted Oxford graduates styled Milner's *Kindergarten*. From being one of Milner's secretaries, Curtis had become secretary of the Commission for the Constitution of Johannesburg, before taking up the post of Town Clerk of the city. It was in that role that he crossed swords with Charles.

Curtis thought he had no more ado than require the Crown Titles Office to surrender Crown Land to the Municipality for its purposes. The Registrar vehemently assured him otherwise. That was not the function of the Crown Titles Office. The Municipality would have to find and purchase sites for itself.

Initial hostility, however, mellowed to mutual regard as each came to know and to appreciate the worth of the other. They became colleagues on the first Financial Relations Commission and both were chosen to exercise progressively greater administrative responsibilities. From such unlikely beginnings, then, friendship grew. Charles was never one to harbour malice.

On the contrary, he sought always the best in a man. In the case of another expatriate, William Dalrymple, an almost exact contemporary (20.9.1864–20.6.1941), and Charles, it seemed that friendship was fore-ordained. Born in Stirlingshire, Dalrymple began his business career at 18 with an accountancy firm in London, before tales of gold strikes drew him to South Africa. Arriving in Klerksdorp in the Far West Rand in 1888, he settled in Johannesburg in 1892 and came to play a significant part in the world of mining on the Rand. A founder of the Johannesburg Caledonian Society, Dalrymple helped raise a volunteer regiment, the South African Scottish Horse, of which he was Commanding Officer with the rank of lieutenant-colonel from 1902 until 1907. Certainly in the first, and probably in both of these projects, Charles also took a prominent part. In the aftermath of the Boer War, he maintained his zeal for matters military by helping to create the Transvaal Scottish Volunteer Regiment. A photograph (circa 1904) shows 'G' Company on parade, 45 strong, resplendent in regalia, including kilts of Murray tartan, under the command of Captain Charles Murray. Dalrymple is even credited with persuading Charles to furnish verses for Caledonian Society dinners. According to Charles Christie, *To the Hin'most Man*, later to appear in the 1917 collection of poems, *A Sough o' War*, owes its creation to Dalrymple's importunity. The following is a sample of the kind of "occasional" offering that Charles could deliver on demand, linking native and adopted countries:

> Here's to the Land o' the Bens and Valleys.
>   Here's to the Land o' the whaups and whins.
> This nicht at least we'll forget our "Sallies"[1]
>   An' dirk the man says a word o' "Tins."[2]

---

[1] "Sallies", [2] "Tins": contemporary Stock Exchange tokens in South Africa

'G' Company, Transvaal Scots Volunteer Regiment,
under the command of Captain Charles Murray – front left (1904–05)

CHAPTER 9

The Work, Woes and Wiles
of a Public Servant

'To the wearimost ends o' the earth again,
An' the wark that is waitin' there.'

Furth Again

The granting by Britain of colonial self-government to the Transvaal in 1906 and the Orange Free State the following year placed them on the same footing as Cape Colony and Natal and paved the way for the creation in 1910 of the Union of South Africa, a self-governing entity within what was in those days the British Empire. Until then each colony had had its own public works authority. On union, all public works and other property in the possession of the four colonies were vested in the Governor-General-in-Council. Management of these government buildings was thereupon entrusted to a Public Works Department expressly set up for the purpose.

For the post of Secretary of Public Works, Union of South Africa, there was only one possible candidate, only one who had the skill, the breadth of experience, the determination, the single-mindedness to integrate the four diverse Public Works Departments of the four constituent colonies. That one was – Charles Murray. At the stroke of a pen the extent of his public works territory exploded from some 110,000 square miles to over 470,000 square miles – five times the area of the United Kingdom. The pen was in the hand of Herbert John, 1st Viscount Gladstone and first Governor-General of the Union of South Africa who, on 22 June 1910, signified his approval of Minute No: 295 emanating from the Prime Minister's Office, Pretoria, couched in the following terms:

Ministers have the honour to recommend that, in accordance with the provisions of Section 15 of the South Africa Act, 1909, of the Imperial Parliament, His Excellency the Governor-General may be pleased to approve of the appointment of Charles Murray Esquire,

as Acting Secretary for Public Works of the Union of South Africa:
the appointment to have effect as from the 31st day of May 1910.

Unifying South Africa was a colossal undertaking, politically and
administratively. For Charles it entailed harmonizing the disparate prac-
tices of the Public Works Departments of the four constituent colonies,
bringing them under his supervision, and to a large extent bringing them
into line with procedures he had successfully introduced into the
Transvaal during his Secretaryship there.

The Public Service lists of the period make interesting reading. Of 28
post-union Works Department officers whose service in the grade
quoted began in April 1912, no fewer than 23 were drawn from the
former Transvaal PWD. Admittedly they were already on the spot when
appointments were made, but they must have been judged capable of
performing at national as distinct from provincial level. In creating this
departmental team, Charles had again demonstrated the justice of
Captain Ogilvie's 1888 assessment of him: "He possesses in a remarkable
degree the faculty of getting men to work at their best and in the best
spirit."

The union of 1910 presented challenges and opportunities not only
for Charles Murray but for Kent-born architect Herbert – later Sir
Herbert – Baker. Resident in South Africa since 1892, Baker had through
a highly-placed family connection in Cape Town been brought to the
favourable attention of many prominent men, among them Cecil J
Rhodes, Prime Minister of Cape Colony. It is said that Rhodes took to
Baker because of the latter's somewhat taciturn nature. "He doesn't talk
too much" was the Prime Minister's approving evaluation.

Rhodes gave him a commission to restore his house, "Groote
Schuur", which had been burnt down. This was the beginning of a
staunch and rewarding friendship. The two had much in common: a
passion for Africa and its panoramic vistas; and a vision of creating architectural masterpieces that would perpetuate their names.

Wide as Baker's professional training had been, Rhodes perceived that
he lacked knowledge of classic architecture and sent him to study in
Egypt, Greece and Italy. This exposure had a profound impact upon the
style of Baker's subsequent work.

The death of Rhodes in 1902, coupled with an invitation from Lord
Milner to practise in the Transvaal at this stimulating post-war period of

Public Servant Charles Murray in formal attire,
following a *levée*, Pretoria (c. 1910)

reconstruction, drew Baker from Cape Town to Johannesburg. During the decade he spent in the Transvaal, Baker set the building profession upon a sound footing, introduced many innovations and excelled in every type of architecture – domestic, ecclesiastical, medical, business, educational, public. The years leading up to the creation of the Union of South Africa presented Baker with his finest architectural opportunities, culminating in 1910 in the Union Buildings, Pretoria, his greatest achievement. A new type of imperial architecture, along classical lines, had emerged.

Cape Town had been selected as the Union's legislative capital, while Pretoria was designated administrative capital. In the latter, therefore, accommodation had to be constructed on a scale and with befitting dignity to house the officers of the four provincial Public Services now integrated. The response was the Union Buildings – Baker's in conception, in execution Charles Murray's. At the laying of the foundation stone by the Governor-General, HRH the Duke of Connaught, at 12.30 pm on Saturday, 26 November 1910, Charles and his wife were very properly among the officially invited guests of the Administration of the Province of Transvaal.

For his masterpiece Baker had chosen an ideal site on Meintjeskop, highest and most prominent of the hills encircling Pretoria, yet no more than a mile from the town centre. Two large identical blocks of administrative offices, each with central courtyard, are linked by a semi-circular, colonnaded building having adjacent to it twin domed towers and facing an open-air amphitheatre. The whole overlooks terraced gardens with fountains and trees, through which winds a road, affording a suitable formal context.

Something has already been said of Charles Murray's appearance. Herbert Baker was no less impressive. A tall man of robust build, arresting in looks as in character, he had below bushy eye-brows dark, deep-set eyes with unwavering gaze. While "taciturn" may have applied to Baker, it is not a word that one would employ about Charles. Circumstances, however, obliged the two to work together and this they did amicably enough as far as can be ascertained, each determined to fight his own professional corner. Baker would countenance no relaxation in standards of design, while Charles saw his prime responsibility as keeping within his Parliamentary budget. This might have generated antagonism had either lacked principle, forthrightness or sense. Recognising the other's virtues, however, each saw the wisdom of co-operation. So far as the Union Buildings were concerned, Charles contrived to satisfy Baker's requirements without over-running his budget or compromising on quality.

The *Annual Report* of the integrated Public Works Department for 1911, published 19 April 1912, at Pretoria, makes interesting reading. While indicating the size and scope of the work done overall, it singles out for especial mention the Union Buildings, as well it might. At a contract price of £878,724, these were the largest and costliest of the Department's undertakings.

Under the heading 'UNION BUILDINGS' the Report records:

"Very satisfactory progress falls to be reported during the year under review… there is reason to anticipate that occupation… may be obtained sooner than at one time appeared possible.

It may be noted here that the erection of these buildings – the Amphitheatre Block and the Eastern and Western Blocks – will require approximately:

       14,000,000 bricks
       500,000 cu.ft. of freestone
       74,000 cu.yds. of concrete
       40,000 bags of cement
       20,000 cu.ft. of granite.

There are 88 cranes on the site, 15 of these worked by electricity: three by steam and the remainder by hand. European operatives to the number of 465 and natives to the number of 800 are employed by contractors. Some 98 white men are engaged in tree-planting, road-making etc."

Under 'ARCHITECTURAL SECTION', it was disclosed that the Drawing Office Staff in Pretoria had performed "the architectural work for all Union and Provincial services," requiring nearly 66,000 prints of drawings. The same section covers the enormous demands imposed in having to compile a Buildings Register embracing the whole Union. Here, as in other fields, the Transvaal PWD had shown the way.

The Report states:

"The Buildings Registry has been engaged in extending to the other

Provinces of the Union the system which was inaugurated in the Transvaal some few years ago. The capital involved in Government Buildings, throughout the Union, amounts, in round figures, to £13,000,000. The buildings are recorded in 3,318 groups, situated as follows:

> Transvaal – 1,371   Cape – 709
> Natal – 628   Orange Free State – 610"

Comprehensive information on each "group" was held on cards, listing such details as:

> "Title under which site is held;
> General description and construction of buildings;
> Date of completion and original cost;
> Cost of repairs and maintenance.

The Transvaal buildings were practically all recorded prior to Union, but in the other Colonies no definite system appears to have been followed. A large amount of work is therefore involved in compiling plans and obtaining information, especially in regard to the older buildings, in order that one uniform system of registration may apply throughout the Union."

Charles saw the wisdom of standardisation in bridge design too, as the Report indicates: "An examination of bridges in the different Provinces showed that there was considerable diversity in such matters as 'loading', type of girders, material used, road width, side walk, etc… It was thought that, though uniformity of practice had not been obtained in the past, some degree of uniformity might be reached, under Union, in the near future and a few standard types might be designed… standardising… will tend to reduce the cost of bridge construction."

Recognition of the Transvaal's exemplary role came also from above. The Report continues: "During the latter part of 1910 Cabinet decided that the accounting work of the Department should be organised on the lines previously adopted in the Transvaal and this was carried out during the year 1911… Some differences still exist in the old accounts of the Cape, Free State and Natal… The difficulty in tracing these differences is enhanced by the absence of necessary detailed information, items having in many cases been debited or credited to our account without supporting schedules or sufficient information. The following figures indicate roughly the amount of work passing through the Office in the ten months ending 31 March 1911:

> Expenditure   £1,468,019.17.1
> Bills and vouchers dealt with numbered   14,388."

Construction undertaken or in progress during the year under review embraced all four Provinces, the Transvaal accounting for nearly a half, while the others had between 9% and 25%. The work ranged from an observatory dome and telescope tower, through schools, Post and Telegraph Offices, police barracks, law courts and library, museums and bridges, to government buildings, culminating in the Union Buildings, Pretoria.

This enormous output and the administrative groundwork that preceded it placed heavy demands upon Charles, demands that he hints at in a letter to his close friend in Aberdeen, George Walker. It indicates too the extent of his responsibilities.

'I got back from Cape Town yesterday,' he writes, 'after nearly six months absence save a fortnight at Christmas. I am mighty glad to be back and to have got over the Parliamentary worries. We got our Estimates through rather easily after all. My Minister has gone home now for three months to the coronation (of King George V) and I have bags of worry before me. We have about two millions to spend on Public Works and to organize the new Department at the same time. Just at present I have a very fierce battle on with the Provincial Administration of the Orange Free State but it is just possible I can hold my own...

I got a little golf at Cape Town but don't improve... I fear I won't have much time to play now, though we have got a fine new 18-hole course laid down at Pretoria. I missed my trout fishing too this year – bad luck to it.

As soon as I get things going here a bit, I will have to knock around a lot, going to Natal first. By this time next year I will either be sacked or wanting a holiday home badly.'

Then follows an insight into his view of himself and his management skills: 'One thing is I am lazy myself and make others work which in a job like mine is a good principle to work on. The man who was PWD Secretary at the Cape tried to do everything himself with fatal results…'

As for Charles, his executive style and its outcomes must have found favour. Far from being "sacked", he was confirmed in the post of "Secretary for Public Works of the Union of South Africa: the appointment to have effect as from 31 May 1910." Confirmation came in response to Minute No. 2092, issuing from the Prime Minister's Office, Pretoria, on 9 January 1912, over the signature of Louis Botha, former commander-in-chief of Boer forces in the Second Boer War, now first premier of the Union of South Africa.

CHAPTER 10

Friends and Foes

'Ye're hardly hame till furth again'
Furth Again

As 1912 progressed, the demands upon Charles Murray doubtless increased, intensifying his longing for home leave. Not until mid-August, however, can it be confidently asserted that he was back on British soil. From a rented house in North Devon, where he is accompanied by his wife and family, he writes to George Walker enquiring about the possibility of accommodation for his wife, himself, their two daughters and a servant at Cruden Bay in October, and giving his subsequent address as Bedford Road, Clapham.

His exact whereabouts on the evening of Monday, 2 December 1912, can be stated with absolute certainty. He was guest of honour at a complimentary dinner in the *Palace Hotel*, Aberdeen, attended by a distinguished company. In the Chair was Professor – later Sir – Ashley W Mackintosh, pre-eminent not only in the field of medicine, but an MA with First Class Honours in Classics and Mathematics. Professor Mackintosh recalled his meetings with their celebrated visitor in Pretoria the previous year, particularly at a dinner of the Aberdeen University Club of South Africa.

The toast to the guest of honour was proposed by the Editor of Aberdeen University Review, Alexander Mackie, who in verses of his own surmised the motivation, the purposes and the potential aftermath of Charles Murray's homecoming:

> He missed the heather, missed the peat,
> He wearied for the Leochel Burn,
> He missed the kindly snaw an' sleet;
> An' syne hamewith he beet to turn.

I met him daunderin' doon the howe
His een explorin' ilka neuk,
An' od! I thocht, "he's stappin's pow
Wi' picters for anither beuk."

He cracks awa' wi' pawky chiels,
An' daffs wi' a' the sonsy queynes,
An' fegs, their unco words he sheels
Red-het into his skeely lines.

His heid's well plenisht noo, I'm seer,
An' ance his fit's on Afric's shore
He'll screed ye, gin he binna swear,
Packmen an' whistlin' herds galore.

In his response, Charles likened himself to the author of *The Frontiersman,* "cursed by two things – a long nose that led him into adventure, and a weak chin that prevented him from carrying through the adventure successfully," adding, 'how great an adventure it is for a simple man from the back veld to get up in front of a gathering like this.' Among the guests was Anthony McCreadie, his former dominie from Gallowhill School, prompting the speaker to say, 'I am unduly conscious that my old schoolmaster is in the room. I have long ago forgiven the hidings he gave me – and he gave me many – and classed them with other benefits I received at his hands. Still I have an uneasy feeling I am on the floor before him again, and, as usual, ill prepared.' Unaccustomed as "a poor public servant" to receiving praise, Charles admitted: 'All these nice things Mr Mackie has said rather take me aback.' Since he believed it the duty of individuals to achieve through their own endeavours, he characterized 'free libraries, free education, philanthropic millionaires (as) three things I equally detest.' Laughter greeted this disclosure.

His use of Scots as the medium of his writing, Charles explained as follows: 'I wrote (in Scots) for two reasons – good reasons, I thought. I think so still. One was that to throw one's mind into the old times and scenes seemed to give me something of an emotional relief, and to open up a happy loophole of retreat from the wear and bustle of colonial life. The other reason was that (the verses) gave pleasure to an old man in the Vale of Alford.' (Peter Murray, his father) 'That these things should be written in the vernacular was neither accidental nor intentional. It was simply inevitable. If I had been forced to, or tried to write in English, I certainly could have done nothing... I have often heard wonder expressed that I should remember the old words, but the wonder to me would be if I could ever forget them.'

'I was raised upon Ramsay, Fergusson and Burns, and the old Scots,' the speaker continued, 'and all my life as a boy I was taught to look out for quaint phrases, out-of-the-way expressions, and to study and delight in the old original characters of the countryside... Suckling said that Carew's verses "were seldom brought forth without trouble and pain." Mine never are, and I find now when I come home at night after a hard day, I am not looking for fresh trouble or pain which can be evaded; instead of hunting for a pen or pencil, I am searching for a pipe, so I am rather afraid I am not likely to carry my vernacular sketches much further.' The year was 1912.

The warmth of the company, Charles admitted, 'has removed a certain shamefacedness from which I have suffered until now. I have always had a feeling that a man might raise chrysanthemums, or even play the flute in his spare time, and still have claims to be considered a good business man, but that if his weakness was rhyming he would at once be set down as a "feckless" character... I have hitherto tried to conceal my weakness from my business associates, or, if they did get to know of it, I tried to pass off these verses of mine as youthful indiscretions.'

It was an evening for benevolent gestures. Upon the call of the Chair, Mr Robert Anderson proposed "in complimentary terms" the health of Mr McCreadie on the twofold counts of educating Mr Murray and originating from the land of Burns. Warm applause, endorsing the toast, was renewed when Anthony McCreadie rose to respond.

'It is some 39 years, or rather more,' said the 67-year-old dominie, 'since I first met Charlie Murray, then a loon of 10 or 11 years. I was living in the house with Mr Murray's father and am glad I have been able to keep my sometime pupil's personal friendship towards myself during all these years. At no time has Mr Murray ever come back to Alford but he makes a point of calling to see his former schoolmaster.'

'I do not know,' continued Mr McCreadie, 'that I would be justified in calling to mind incidents of bygone days in connection with the early career of Charlie Murray.' Cries of "No, no," laughter and applause approved this tactful evasion. 'I have frequently had the pleasure,' disclosed Mr McCreadie, 'of seeing Mr Murray's poems before they were published. He often sent home to his father the first rough drafts. Mr Murray, as a poet, got more from heredity than from his schoolmaster, because the miller, his uncle, used to like poetry. It is quite true, as Mr Murray has represented, that the miller had "aye a sid in his throat." The miller had a very fine collection of old songs, and could write, and Mr Murray's father himself has been guilty of rhyming too,' a revelation greeted with applause.

'I am very glad,' Mr McCreadie concluded, 'Mr Murray's health is now so good. It is told that when he went out first to South Africa, he was known among the Kaffirs as "the man with the cough." We all hope that when he goes back there he will retain his health and continue to prosper.' These sentiments drew loud applause.

Writing from Edinburgh to George Walker a few days after the genial occasion just described, Charles had news he was eager to share: 'I have had such a fine letter from Gavin Greig' (the collector of Scots folk songs). 'He is giving away only two other copies' (of his book *Folk Song of the North East*, then in course of publication): one to Charles, one to his friend of long-standing, Dr James Tocher. 'It is mighty good of him but everyone has been so confoundedly kind that I am in danger of taking it all as a matter of course.'

Charles was perhaps beginning to appreciate the enormous affection in which he was held and rightly held, and with the self-deprecating attitude typical of the North-east could not accept it as justified. Sadly, Gavin Greig did not live to keep his pledge in person, but his widow saw to it that in due course his collaborator, the Reverend James Bruce Duncan, sent the promised gift to Charles in Pretoria.

That conclusion, however, was some years ahead. By mid-December 1912, his leave at an end, Charles was in Southampton about to embark once more for South Africa. "Just off," he telegraphed home, "goodbye love to all the Boys and Girls. Murray."

He had, one hopes, found his furlough restful and revitalizing, for a daunting work-load confronted him on his return. Writing from Pretoria to George Walker in July 1913, he admits: 'I was seedy pretty well all the time I was in Cape Town and had plenty of worry as well while Parliament was sitting and I never had any energy to do anything in the evenings. Now I am back on the high veld I am picking up. I began to think I was getting old and finished (he was in his 49th year) but I have still a little kick left and during the strike (of miners) turned out with a rifle and 30 rounds to do Policeman duty. A mad thing it was to arm a lot of all sorts and turn them into the street, a nuisance too – it interfered with my Sunday golf.

Everyone and everything here is pretty unsettled. I expect any day to be told by the Treasury to go slow with new works and I shall be glad

Charles Murray caught at shipboard exercise *en route* for South Africa, December 1912
Courtesy The Kinfauns Kastle Kronikle

to be told it too, for we have an enormous programme before us: about 2 millions to spend on buildings and bridges and all plans to be made in one office, and three months of the financial year gone.'

As the civil servant heading the Public Works Department, Charles had to apportion his time between overseeing progress on a vast range of Government construction, and appearing before Parliamentary bodies to justify his requirements or expenditure. This involved shuttling between public service HQ in Pretoria and the seat of legislation in Cape Town. He had a poor opinion of politicians and privately savoured encounters where he carried his point. This comes across in a letter of his of 1 May 1914 from Cape Town. It reads in part: 'I had a run up to Pretoria for a week to see how my office was getting on. I expect I will be here (i.e. The Cape) for another 2 months yet, a very tedious business. I had two full days of the Accounts Committee but don't think they pulled much wool off me. The great thing is to appear to be absolutely frank and at the same time not to tell them more than is convenient. Now I have to prepare for the defence of my Estimates in Parliament. The trouble there is you have to get the Minister to answer the questions which is less satisfactory than if you could do it yourself. I seldom see my Minister in these days: he is so busy with political affairs and lets me run on my own, which is all very well as long as things go right but he does not know the risks he takes of being let down.' He adds: 'I am going to sneak off tomorrow for a day's golf with Patrick Duncan' – a Scot who rose to high political office in South Africa.

On a subsequent occasion he confides: 'I am having a very lazy time just now but next week have to face the Accounts Committee, about 20 MPs – all financial pundits – who examine me on my accounts of two years ago, an operation which calls for all your wits, especially if you want to throw dust in their eyes.'

Presently, however, there was more to occupy Charles than parliamentary skirmishes or tussles on fairway and green.

CHAPTER 11

A Sough o' War

'The loon an' me had sodgered wi' the rest'

The Thraws o' Fate

By August 1914 the world was at war, hostilities that not only engulfed Europe but spread even to southern Africa. Charles became concerned in both theatres of conflict, not on his own account but on that of his son, Bill, a 17-year-old schoolboy at Loretto, Midlothian, a member of the school Shooting VIII and a Corporal in the Officer Training Contingent.

Some months earlier, learning that Bill was contemplating a career in engineering, Charles had imparted fatherly advice and personal admissions. 'It is not an easy life you are planning for yourself,' he writes, '
If you go to Aberdeen you will have the advantage of having some friends. When I went in there at your age I knew nobody but I always made friends of men better than myself, and if I could not get good company, I kept to myself... don't be put off by a rough exterior... manners is not everything. It is character which counts all the time... you need not fear to open your heart and mind to me. Remember I have gone through all the anxiety, the worry and the temptations myself and know how to sympathise with them.'

The closing paragraph reveals the man's humanity and humility: 'I suppose the young men in my office look upon me as rather a big man with an assured position but, tho' I perhaps don't show it, I am just as anxious about myself as they are about themselves, and often get discouraged and blame myself for not doing my work as well as I might and ought, and I expect I will go on like that to the end, never doing as well as I would like to but always trying to do better... '

Although approaching his half-century, Charles was eager to play an active part in hostilities and sought repeatedly through influential contacts for a combatant role. In this, to his intense disappointment, he was unsuccessful.

As early as January 1915, Charles was briefing George Walker on the military situation in his territory: 'Things are getting in train for the German South West (Africa) campaign. Report says we will have 70,000 under arms in which case it may not last long.'

Charles continued to be greatly exercised over his son's future. Bill's schooling was to end in April and the road ahead appeared to lead inexorably towards the forces, either in Europe with the Royal Engineers – "the pick of the army" in his father's partisan view – or in the Artillery, bound for South West Africa. In the event, the boy served in both war zones. According to a letter of his father's, he was due to sail for "German West" on 26 May 1915. He would have seen out hostilities there, much to the envy of his father who made persistent but ineffectual efforts to share the action in that quarter: 'I am still trying to get to German South West before the campaign finishes. My Minister has at last agreed that I can go if wanted and the Defence Department has wired to General Botha to see if he can use me. Probably he can't but if I can get up in a Civil capacity I might manage to get a shot at the blighters somehow. Fox (a colleague)… was in charge of his Regiment in the only engagement they were *lucky enough*★ to get into" – a telling phrase.

By early August fighting in "German West" was at an end. So far as his son was concerned, Charles did not know what the future held. 'I expect he will go back to Europe by and by,' he confided in a letter to George Walker, 'though whether to France or with the heavy Artillery to the Dardanelles I can't decide yet.'

That letter was closely followed by another, giving in typically laconic fashion the latest news: 'I will probably be off to German South West, the newly conquered territory, this week… I have some 25 men still in GSW, amongst them my Chief Architect… and my Chief Electrician. I have a wire from them yesterday asking me to go up and arrange for future working now war is over and the Chief Secretary for the new Civil Administration followed with a wire today to the same effect. I suppose they really think they want me but probably they also thought I would not be averse to a trip through the new country.'

Not until 6 October 1915 do we learn that Bill Murray, perhaps granted a spell of leave with his parents, had already left their home in Pretoria to report to Potchefstroom, some 100 miles distant. Charles and

---

★ present writer's italics

Mary Robbie, 'faithful friend and housckeeper' of Peter Murray for 47 years,
in the doorway of *Murrayfield*, Alford, his home in retirement,
where she died on 21 April 1915, aged 75

Edith were intending to travel down to the camp there to say their farewells as his contingent was to sail for Europe about October 15.

Despite their abiding anxiety over their son, Charles was not unmindful of his ageing father, bereft since her death on 21 April 1915, of the companionship of his sister-in-law, Mary Robbie, who had, quite literally, devoted her life to looking after him. In a letter of 11 November 1915 to George Walker, Charles ventures a suggestion: 'I heard a gramophone the other night which made me wonder if one would cheer and amuse my old father in the winter nights... It is perhaps not times to buy things of that sort, but anything that makes him less lonely is worth doing.'

The gift was duly bought and proved a great success as Charles presently reports, acknowledging the help of George's wife in making the purchase: 'I am very obliged to Bella for seeing about the gramophone. The old man is very pleased with it and perhaps it will be some company for him.'

Thoughts of his father may have prompted in Charles recollections of the turn of the century, when he himself went off to the Boer War, leaving wife and young family. On that occasion "the old man" had not sought to deflect him. Nor was Charles in his turn disposed to place barriers in Bill's path to military service. Denied the opportunity to "have a crack at the enemy", Charles felt pride in having a boy who knew where his duty lay. Far from being indifferent, Charles was keenly aware of the possible consequences and of the constant dread endured by parents in their situation.

Relaying to Bella Walker the news that he had had a cable informing him that Bill was in France, Charles continues: 'Edith gets very weepy over it, but as I ask her how would she have felt if he hadn't wanted to go. The whole thing is too big for personal feelings to come in. One must just be philosophic and trust that he will come through.'

To bear arms in defence of his homeland: that Charles saw as the manifest duty of a patriot. He went so far as to disown a relative who had chosen to marry a conscientious objector. His own superiors, however, judged that the most significant contribution he could make lay in his administrative expertise. In July 1916, therefore, he found himself involved at the behest of the South African Government in the question of employment for legions of returning servicemen.

As if additional professional duties and concerns over his son's safety were not burdens enough, towards the end of 1916, in letters addressed to Bella Walker, Charles reports: 'The family is in trouble this week. Edith in a nursing home with appendicitis … Her brother (William, a surgeon) got across before the operation but the local surgeon did it.' A postscript the following day adds: 'She seems to have got a touch of jaundice… she blames their medicines and has taken her treatment into her own hands.'

Just over a week later, he is able to give the reassuring news: 'Edith is getting on fine…' but goes on to refer to another family member also on the sick list: 'Heard yesterday from my brother-in-law in German East Africa. He had just had his 8th go of fever so he may possibly be invalided home with a lot who are expected back before Xmas.' This was Andrew Reid, husband of Charles's sister, Sarah, like him resident in South Africa. The "lot… expected back before Xmas" consisted largely 'of returned soldiers, some 8000… arriving from German East, rotten with fever and dysentery' for whose reception 'our Defence Department has made a hash of the hospital arrangements.'

On a more personal plane, perhaps as an outlet for thwarted martial ambitions, Charles had embarked after a somewhat fallow period on a series of poems on aspects of war. Some appeared initially in periodicals or newspapers, including *The Times*. Resultant fees he donated to military causes. 'By the way,' he writes to Bella Walker, referring to a recent composition, '*Scotland Counts* has now brought £24 to War Funds for permission to reprint which is a little comfort – only a little – to a man who is too old to fight.'

In spite of distractions, the accumulation of verse grew. Encouraged by favourable comment, Charles was persuaded to have the collection published in book form. Again it was to Constable & Co., London, that he entrusted publication. Not until mid-June 1917, however, was he able to report to George Walker receipt of the slim volume of 14 pieces, one providing the title – *A Sough o' War*. Its dusky pink jacket brought forth from Charles the exclamation: 'What a bloodsome cover!' Typically, the writer expressed his misgivings over its merit: 'I wonder now if these darned rhymes were worth printing, I doubt it.' The dedication reads:

TO A YOUNG SAPPER
SOMEWHERE IN FRANCE

AND TO ALL IN WHAT-
EVER AIRT UPHOLDING
THE FAIR NAME AND
HONOUR OF SCOTLAND

A father's thoughts were with his son, and with the other defenders of Scotland's freedom.

Although unified by the theme of war, "these strouds o' rhymes", as Charles unassumingly terms them, are diverse in form, in feeling, in tone. They range from the stirring, even jingoistic challenges of the title piece, of *Wha bares a blade for Scotland?* and *To the Hin' most Man*, through the frustration evident in *The Thraws o' Fate*, to the serio-comic *The Wife on the War*. Among the most authentic is the epistle *Fae France*, recreating not only the voice of the North-east, but the complex of relationships among the *dramatis personae*. The sender, no longer "'Sandy" noo, but "Sergeant" Aberdein,' promoted for gallantry, writes from hospital where he is recovering from a wound. He relates how army life suits his aggressive nature:

> There's me, fan but a bairn in cotts, nae big aneuch to herd,
> Would seener steek my nieves an' fecht, than dook or ca' my gird,

belligerence that led him into strife and eventually an appearance before the 'Shirra' who, as it happened, was father of Sandy's future platoon commander. On a successful raid into enemy territory, the officer is wounded and owes his deliverance to Sandy:

> To hyste him up an' on my back nott a' my pith an' skeel,
> For aye he bad' me lat him lie, an' cursed me for a feel.
> "Ging on an' leave me here, ye gype, an' mak' yer feet yer freen'."
> "Na, na," says I; "ye brocht me here, I'm nae gyaun hame my leen."

In a letter of thanks, the officer's mother

> ... speir't could she dae ocht for me, sae I sent back a line –
> "Jist bid yer man, fan neist I'm up, ca' canny wi' the fine."

When kept from sleep by pain, Sandy recalls the scenes and activities of home, lovingly evoked in Charles Murray's verse. This is a very accomplished piece, seeming to flow spontaneously from topic to topic, without sentimentality, self-pity or conceit.

While "Sandy" has longings for home, "Jock" in *Bundle and Go*, that sparkling alliterative gem, can hardly wait to enlist:

> I've focht wi' the weather, the wark an' the weemen,
>   Till faith I'm in fettle for facin' the foe,
> An' waukin' or dreamin' I hear the pipes screamin'
> "Hie, Jock, are ye ready to bundle an' go?"
>   Bundle an' go.
> Wha bides fan the pipes bid him "Bundle an' go"?

Responsive as he was to patriotic summons, Charles Murray was attuned also to the suffering occasioned by war, especially the parting of sweethearts for a term – or for life. In two poems, *At the Loanin' Mou'* and *When Will the War Be By?,* he shows himself particularly sensitive to the sacrifice made by women bereft of their men. The second of these pieces, mimicking the petal-stripping ritual of "He loves me; he loves me not," tiptoes to a desolating close:

> "Weel, wounded, missin', deid,"
>   Is there nae news o' oor lads ava?
>   Are they hale an' fere that are hine awa'?
> A lass raxed oot for the list, to read –
> "Weel, wounded, missin', *deid*";
>   An' the war was by for twa.

In the view of many, the most powerful of the pieces in *A Sough o' War* is undoubtedly the dramatic monologue *Dockens Afore His Peers*, a searing indictment of one man's self-absorption and unwitting self-revelation and a craven tribunal's capitulation. No need for the poet to utter one word of denunciation: Dockens condemns himself and, after delivering a torrent of spurious justification, goes on to skewer the tribunal, blackmailed into granting his workers, in particular his youngest son, immunity from military service, by proposing a celebratory drink:

> "Total Exemption." Thank ye, sirs. Fat say ye till a dram?

By the close, the atmosphere is explosive. The whole is a *tour de force*, assured, dynamic, satisfying in its self-containment.

Scarcely had *A Sough o' War* been published before Charles found himself constrained to respond to a friend's request for a verse contribution to the Jubilee issue of the *Cairngorm Magazine*. The stipulation, as he discloses in a letter to George Walker, was for "something on the Aberdeen Hills or on Benachie" *(sic)*; the response was *Bennachie* which closes with the heartfelt tribute:

> There's braver mountains ower the sea,
> An' fairer haughs I've kent, but still
> The Vale o' Alford! Bennachie!
> Yon is the Howe, an' this the Hill!

'Incidentally,' adds Charles, 'Table Mountain at Cape Town which I hope we will climb together some day rises sheer from the sea and is 3 times the height of Bennachie.' His merry Muse afoot, Charles next shares with George the first stanza and the chorus of a rollicking "Good Night song" he has just begun:

> Noo I've sattled the score, an' the gig's at the door,
>   An' the shaltie is kittle to ca',
> Aye the langer we sit we're the sweirer to flit,
>   Sae it's time to be wearin' awa'.
> A douce eller like me, an example maun be,
>   An' it wouldna be seemly ava'
> Stottin' hame in day-licht, an' jist think o' the sicht
>   Supposin' we happened to fa'.
> Ye're weel-slockened noo, an' afore ye get fou
>   Be guided by me an' say "Na";
> By my tongue ye can tell I've had plenty mysel',
>   Sae a cheery guid-nicht to you a'.
> A cheery guid-nicht, ay, a cheery guid-nicht,
>   A cheery guid-nicht to you a',
> By my sang ye can tell I've had plenty mysel',
>   Sae a cheery guid-nicht to you a'.

Before the month was out Charles was again writing to George, this time with ill-concealed elation. His hopes of involvement in the war effort were being realised. In August 1917, following an approach by the Quarter Master General, he was gazetted Director of Works, Union Defence Forces, with the rank of Temporary Lieutenant-Colonel.

Lieutenant-Colonel Charles Murray, Director of Works,
South African Defence Force (1917)

Charles felt under something of an obligation to accept the invitation, recalling that the Quarter Master General was 'the chap I came from German West (Africa) with two years ago when we did a record trip from Windhoek to the coast. He is the dearest little chap going, always beaming with good nature and the only one of the Defence crowd I would care to work with.'

The first assignment was a crucial one. 'I am a bit busy,' admitted Charles, 'as we have to run up a large hospital for soldiers at the coast and men and materials are scarce.'

While privately rather proud to be donning uniform, towards which a meagre £10 was allowed, Charles 'could see the disadvantages already. The one that worries me most is the smoking. I always carry ¼lb bag of tobacco and two pipes and I don't see how I can stow that away in a uniform without looking lumpy.' He mentions another – flippant – image concern: 'Then I have to go down to Durban and there is a nurse in the Medical Hospital there I have kissed since she was a girl… I haven't seen her for years and if I kiss her now I can fancy: "Look at that hoary headit buffer of a Colonel mashing[1] the nurse" but I suppose these are the minor discomforts like rats in the trenches.'

Involvement in the war effort, albeit in a non-combatant role, seemed to free Charles's spirit to embark on further verse. The letter of 30 August 1917, to George Walker refers to a 'final' version of *Benachie* (*sic*) and an additional stanza for *A Cheery Guid Nicht*. More significantly, it mentions the death while on active service in France of a young friend, who shared his worship of the countryside. '[It] made me think,' writes Charles, 'of the lots of gallant fellows who loved and tramped the hills who will never see them again. I tried a couple of verses but they don't look quite as if they had come off.'

Not everyone would agree with the poet's modest assessment of the commemorative piece, originally entitled *Laurels fae Lonach* but subsequently published as *In Lythe Strathdon*:

> Seldom a simmer passed but him an' me
> Amang the hills had some fine cheery days,

---

[1] A term originating perhaps in the US, circa 1882, now obsolete, meaning 'exciting sentimental admiration in (one of the opposite sex).' *The Shorter Oxford English Dictionary* [Newnes]

> Up Nochtyside or throu' the Cabrach braes,
> Doon the Lord's Throat, an' ootower Bennachie;
> There wasna mony bare hill-heads onkent to him an' me.

> Never nae mair. I wander noo my leen,
>   An' he's been beddit lang in tar Peronne;
>   Here, whaur his forbears lie in lythe Strathdon,
> I lay the stag-moss that I pu'ed yestreen –
> Laurels fae Lonach, where I range oor auld hill tracks my leen.

Perhaps most poignant is the phrase "Never nae mair", the double negative slowing the pace to numbing finality.

There appeared also in 1917 a new edition of *Hamewith*, retaining the Andrew Lang *Introduction* from the 1909 edition, but illustrated with 51 complementary drawings by A S Boyd, where the earlier edition had had two Douglas Strachan illustrations.

For Charles, his verse was little more than a diversion. Understandably, his thoughts and those of his wife were focused primarily on their son, still serving in France. The further education of their elder daughter, Edythe Margaret, lately turned 18, had also been exercising the minds of the Murrays. From Cape Town Charles wrote to George Walker: '... if she can manage an ordinary degree at St Andrews [University] it would be well. We agreed to St Andrews in preference to Aberdeen because... [of] the advantage of having a bit of residential life.' The Walkers, dwellers in the city, would no doubt have insisted on her living with them had she opted for the University of Aberdeen.

Rarely does Charles divulge the impression he makes on others. His letter of 21 May 1918, to George Walker, again written from Cape Town, where he had been in attendance at parliamentary meetings, is an exception: 'I got my Estimates through the lower House, last week, a good deal of talk but they didn't pull much wool... Merriman, the father of the house – this is his 50th year as a member – and a former Cape premier, referred to me as "the amiable, charming and efficient Head of the Department," which is hardly how I would describe myself. One member crossed the floor at once to chaff me about it and lots of friendly grins were thrown at me by other members."

A few lines later Charles lets slip how he does regard himself in this, his 54th year. 'Edith tells me I must write Bill for his 21st Birthday. Lord, how time passes. We are getting old, I suppose, tho' I find in my case years don't bring wisdom.'

He was still young in spirit, however, for the letter is accompanied by a four-verse frolic entitled *The Golden Age* – '... the result,' he reveals, 'of a remark of one of Lord Buxton's ADC's. He is only 24 and a great lad and he confided in me that the best age for a woman was 32.' The opening and closing stanzas give the flavour:

> I'll leave you the lasses that's still i' their teens,
>   Lang-haired an' reid-cheekit, short-coatit an' a',
> An' maids i' the twenties, tho' cuddlesome queans, –
>   They've mair skeel o' kissing at thirty-an'-twa.

★   ★   ★   ★

> Aul' berries are bitter, young grozarts are green,
>   But mid-wye they're ripe an' the sweetest o' a';
> To kittle, to coort, for a wife or a frien',
>   Gie me the dear deemie that's thirty-an'-twa.

CHAPTER 12

Recuperation and Recognition

'An' it's guid to mind there are frien's behind
Aye wishin' ye weel, – an' back.'

Furth Again

As 1918 advanced, there are indications in his letters to the Walkers
that Charles is yearning for Scotland and regretting that for financial reasons he cannot yet retire, although the option exists. With three
children to educate, he is dependent on the increments of pension from
"a few years more" in post. 'Though I have nothing official,' he
concedes, 'my Minister says he wants me to stay on.'

It was getting on for six years since his last home leave. Nostalgia for
old haunts was allied to concern tinged with guilt over his closest kin. 'I
never hear from my father now. I expect he makes the excuse of his
blindness,' he writes, but admits, 'I am afraid I don't write him so often
as I ought to either.'

Charles had anxieties too about his sister Sarah – Mrs Andrew Reid
– then residing in Kimberley, a victim of the 'flu' epidemic sweeping
South Africa. She had been struck down 'when alone and just lay in bed
until the fever went. Since then she has been working on relief early and
late.'

In Cape Town one tenth of the inhabitants had perished. 'Even in
little Pretoria,' he reports, 'we have buried about 600. Our house kaffir
got it but is over it and I hope the rest of us will escape.'

Charles had once more been trying his hand at verses. One piece he
had recently submitted to George Walker for critical scrutiny was *Isie*
which had met with the latter's approbation. '... glad you approve of it,'
writes Charles. 'I thought myself it was heavy and ragged.'

His readers would dispute this view. The poem, rich in characterization and salted with a somewhat testy humour, is addressed by a jealous
swain to the lady of the title who has seemingly accepted his suit. Isie is
a farm lass so captivating that she sets racing the pulses of all the farm
hands from the young herd to the "auld orra man".

An' syne when the milkin's by, an' the fire-hoose clean,
    An' ye daunder oot for a breath o' the gloamin' air,
Ye dinna get far throu' the stibble or ley your leen,
    The laads are loupin' the dykes to kepp you there.

The horsemen are hingin' about to see you pass,
    The baillie's hairt is duntin' aneth his sark,
The yowes are left to wander at will, my lass,
    There's that aboot *you* that disna gyang weel wi' wark.

Her sweetheart is resentful of the admiration she awakens, envious even of 'the lucky cogue that cuddles aneth (her) airm' as she heads for the byre. Distrustful, he entreats her to honour her pledge to pack and go off with him at the appointed time.

Mention of *Isie* leads Charles to recount how he was lately prompted to resume paraphrasing Horace after receiving from an unnamed American a version which, he observes, fell below that of Marris, his classical scholar friend.

'I don't know if you are interested in Horace,' he writes to George Walker, 'but it is wonderful how modern in spirit the old poet is. This *Ode* is to the effect that the gods are of some account after all and that it is just as well to come to terms with them.'

Horace Car. I, 34 Parcus deorum, in paraphrase, is a fine instance of how Charles is able to capture the intent of the original while substituting contemporary images, here from the closing stages of World War I or from the Russian Revolution.

An' ower the sea it's waur than that.   The Marne is rinnin' reid,
The lang canals an' saughy burns are dammed wi' German deid;
An' bonny Wipers, braw Louvain, an' France's fairest touns,
Cathedrals, hospitals an' a' are levelled to the founs.

But noo the Kaiser an' his Kings are skirtin' fae the lan';
They seen got youkie roon the chouks when God put tee a han';
An' Fortune like an aeroplane comes loupin' doon the blue,
An' kills a Czar to place in pooer some raggit Russian Jew.

The letter closes with a rare reference to Charles's health: 'I still play a little so-called golf... Lord I would like a week at Cruden Bay I beleive (*sic*) it might even put my innards right again.'

By the end of 1918 Charles was able to write from Pretoria to George Walker: '... my military duties are very light now and I still wear uniform just because it is thrifty to do so. I hope it will last out until Bill returns so that he will have to salute me at the station. These young bloods will be so full of themselves they will be inclined to patronise their old fathers.'

Looking ahead to the new year, he continues: 'Then by the end of January I will have to move to Cape Town for the (Parliamentary) Session. Lord, how I hate politics and politicians with their dodging and compromise.' A month into the Session his mood of disenchantment had not lifted. 'Living in the (Civil Service) Club and very tired of it,' he writes to George. 'Lord, how I hate politics. I can't understand any man going into it... I wish I could afford to take my pension this year.'

On the positive side, however, he is able to report, 'I have had very nice letters from Defence Department and from my immediate chief, the Quarter Master General, about the work we have done for them which surprised me as a Public Works Department never gets any credit but plenty of abuse.'

A few days earlier, in a letter to Bella Walker, Charles had written: 'I hope Edith will go home at the end of the year and I hope I will follow this time next year unless we have new elections here and things get in a mess.'

Rather less than two months later this projection has been revised. 'I hope to see you all in Aberdeen this year,' says Charles, 'though I haven't suggested it to my Minister yet. Next year we will have a new Parliament and there won't be much chance of getting away when I have another Minister to educate. My present man I hardly ever see. He just lets me do as I like so long as I keep him out of trouble and so far I have been lucky – or he has.'

By late June 1919, plans for home leave were taking shape. 'We hope to sail by the *Llanstephan (Castle)* about the end of July. We hardly realize it yet and Edith, partly the result of the 'flu', is sure something will happen to stop us. I hope not. I am now trying to get a lease on our house so that we can let it and save having to pack and store.'

Edith's fears proved unfounded: the Murrays *did* journey back to UK late summer or early autumn, 1919. Not until 10 October, however, from a letter to Bella Walker, does it emerge that in taking leave Charles was in quest of health as well as rest and relaxation. Evidently the problem with his "innards", which a year previously he had thought a week's golf at Cruden Bay would remedy, had persisted. Indeed it resulted in his having to spend several weeks undergoing tests and treatment as an in-patient at Duff House, Banff, former home of the Duke and Duchess of Fife, but at that period enjoying renown as a sanatorium.

A magnificent early-18th-century edifice, set in the gently undulating Deveron Valley, Duff House had briefly been an hotel before conversion to a sanatorium, specialising in "the scientific investigation and treatment of disorders of nutrition," including colitis, dyspepsia, habitual constipation, tropical disorders and ulceration, but excluding "inebriation". Run by Dr (subsequently Sir) Edmund Ivens Spriggs, the sanatorium had in view an affluent clientele. In addition to the 15 guineas a week charge for treatment, accommodation ranged from 18 to 30 guineas weekly. Exclusive use of a bathroom cost another guinea.

Not only the tariff but the strictness of the medical regime brought protests from Charles. In letters to the Walkers he complained: 'I am cut down to a smoke after meals so I count afternoon tea a meal, but what is 4 smokes a day to one accustomed to 40?... They are still photographing my interior. They must have enough to start a cinema by now... I am a little better I think but had rather a bad night which annoys me as I want to get away from this... Did I tell you I had knocked off smoking? Haven't had a pipe for 10 days. I miss it of course but I want to give myself every chance... I have to lie down 12–1 and 6–7 and bed at 10 and can't go out to meals or have you here... When the Asst Dr saw me today, he said he would rather wait the Snr's return and let him tell me what was wrong. He said I could congratulate myself that they had discovered the trouble with practically no dubiety... I fancy there is nothing serious and hope it is just chronic indigestion... a waste of time and money... I hope to leave on Tuesday, not quite better but I can't afford more time and money.'

In the course of his incarceration Charles, sociable as ever, had made the acquaintance of a Mr Hay with whom he went visiting in the locality. He even entertained patients and staff with stories. 'We have some amusing chatter,' he confides. 'One way or another I try to keep myself and some others cheerful but it is heavy going especially in this weather.' The surroundings, however, were inviting. One day he reports, 'Had a great walk to Brig o' Alvah.' This picturesque bridge, built in 1772, spans the River Deveron some two miles SSW of Duff House, giving access to former family property. A little way to the north of the house stands the Barnyards, the one-time stable-block. Between 1913 and 1923, while the house was a sanatorium, the block became a nurses' home. It would doubtless tickle Charles to know that today the Barnyards are part of Duff House Royal Golf Club.

Discharged at length from the sanatorium, Charles found he was not yet at liberty to return to South Africa. He had been asked by the South African High Commissioner, London, to defer his departure in order to advise on the purchase of a central site in the capital for a "South Africa House" at a cost of about half a million and a rental of £30,000 per annum.

He could see advantages in delay. From the High Commission, Westminster, he writes to George Walker: 'I hope to get a cabin to myself in the new boat (the Union Castle Line *RMS Norman*) which is better. Then he (the High Commissioner) has to pay my expenses here; so I move into a hotel today.'

On quite other grounds postponement of his return was opportune. Although his previous volume of verses, *A Sough o' War*, was not yet three years old, his creative impulse had not lain dormant. He had gradually been garnering a store of pieces: some pre-dating, but unsuited for, his last collection; some originally published in various periodicals.

To publish this new selection he had again engaged Constable and Company Ltd., London. His being there would have made communication speedier and more convenient. In the letter just alluded to, he reveals something of the manoeuvring that accompanies commercial deals, incidentally manifesting his own business acumen. '(Constables) offered an advance against the new book (the future *In the Country Places*) but I refused. They have sold 1700 of the Cheap Edition (i.e. of *Hamewith*) and have no copies left and only supplied Scotland. They are to publish the new book in about 3 mos. They spoke of putting the two old books and this new stuff in one book... but I said give the new one a run first... The new one will be 3/6 and I get 20% = 8½d a copy.' Charles declined to allow a photograph of himself to be included.

In the Country Places comprises 26 poems, demonstrating once more his versatility of topic and treatment. Humour there is and reflection, sentimental or philosophical, economy in description, realistic characterization. To the present writer's mind, the best would encompass: *It*

Wasna His Wyte; Still, Man, Still; Gin I Was God; Isie; Yokin' the Mear; The Tinkler; and, although they are paraphrases, *Heraclitus* and *Horace, Car.I, 9.* There is about them a satisfying sense of completeness that any addition or abridgment would impair.

Publication of this new collection brought praise from a South African government Minister, Patrick Duncan, who also happened to be a North-east Scot. He wrote:

> My Dear Murray
> The post has just brought me *In Country Places (sic)* and it at once wiled me away from other things on which I am supposed to be busy... You seem to me to touch the strings with a firmer hand, more master of your instrument than ever before. It gives me the thrill that is unmistakable but indescribable by which you know the master from the copyist.

Besides finalising details with his publisher, Charles had through the good offices of J M Bulloch, the editor, been introduced to William Will, a Huntly man, Managing Director of *The Graphic.* 'They say they will gladly print anything I send them,' Charles tells George Walker. This was no empty promise. The next letter Charles wrote to George reports: 'Will has been mighty kind to me. Bulloch is printing *A Cheery Guid-Nicht* in *The Graphic.*'

Having obviously, while in London, been in contact with his father's erstwhile employers, Charles goes on to ask a favour of George on their behalf. 'Could you kindly get for me a copy of *Haughton House,* a Strathspey by James Mitchell. I am almost sure it is published separately for the piano. Our Laird Women, the Farquharsons, never heard of it and I said I would get them a copy. If you get one, address it to Miss Farquharson, 17 Moore Street, Cadogan Square, LONDON SW3.' Mindful of his father's many selfless years in the service of the Farquharson family and their grateful recognition of his loyalty, Charles was only too willing to oblige them.

He mentions also the possibility of seeing his sister, Sarah, expected in London shortly. Thanks to his intercession, arrangements for her voyage back to South Africa had been made.

Edith Murray had expressed disappointment at not being there in London, but Charles, with effrontery typical of a man, alleged: 'She wouldn't have enjoyed it as I would hardly have seen her.' Towards the end of his leave, however, she did manage to join him on at least two occasions.

One was a well-attended supper at the London Robert Burns Club on Monday 26 January 1920, chaired by club president William Will, a passionate promoter of Scottish poetry in addition to his professional involvement in publishing. The theme of the evening was "The Bard of Yesterday and Bards of Today". It was appropriate, therefore, that among the company, besides Charles, was the North-east vernacular poet, Violet Jacob, whose creative gifts Charles regarded highly.

'We are most fortunate,' declared the president, 'in having been able to intercept on his way to South Africa Mr Charles Murray, "Hamewith", one of the greatest masters of vernacular poetry that Scotland has produced. Charles Murray is already among the immortals. (Greeted with calls of "Hear, hear!") If he be not in poetic stature the height of Robert Burns, he is still growing. The life of the common people has been the theme of Mr Murray's work, but when he has essayed more ambitious flights of poetic fancy he has touched heights reached only by great poets. The other day he recited to a few friends 16 lines that will live long after the poet has passed to his rest. Mr Murray, his mind full of the horrors of war, of poison gas, exploding shells, atrocities, maimed young bodies, and bruised hearts, put to himself the question – What would he do with the world were he the Deity? And with the reverence of a religious man he recited these lines –

> Gin I was God, sittin' up there abeen,
> Weariet ɪɪae doot noo a' my darg was deen,
> Deaved wi' the harps an' hymns oonendin' ringin',
> Tired o' the flockin' angels hairse wi' singin',
> To some clood-edge I'd daunder furth an', feth,
> Look ower an' watch hoo things were gyaun aneth.
> Syne, gin I saw hoo men I'd made mysel'
> Had startit in to pooshan, sheet an' fell,
> To reive an' rape, an' fairly mak' a hell
> O' my braw birlin' Earth, – a hale week's wark –
> I'd cast my coat again, rowe up my sark,

> An', or they'd time to lench a second ark,
> Tak' back my word an' sen' anither spate,
> Droon oot the hale hypothec, dicht the sklate,
> Own my mistak', an', aince I'd cleared the brod,
> Start a'thing ower again, gin I was God."

While Charles would have writhed under such fulsome praise – and especially on hearing his own work quoted publicly – he not only took part in proceedings by responding to the toast "Scottish Literature", but even forgave William Will his effusive tribute. So began between the two a warm friendship that spanned some 20 years.

The other engagement, a purely private affair two days before Charles sailed, saw the Murrays guests of Lord and Lady Gladstone at dinner. 'A nice kindly pair,' Charles terms them. Herbert John Gladstone had been appointed first Governor-General of the Union of South Africa in 1910. He it was who on 22 June of that year signified approval "in anticipation of the next meeting of the Executive Council" of the appointment of Charles Murray as Acting Secretary for Public Works of the Union of South Africa. His interest in the career of this rising public servant was maintained even to the extent of writing a letter of congratulation on seeing his name appear in the New Year's Honours List for 1922.

That was still two years off. Now, as January 1920 drew to a close, it was time for Charles to bid farewell to Edith who was remaining in UK meantime and to embark on the *Norman* for Cape Town to resume duty.

Despite his costly sojourn in Duff House, Charles had not regained full health and vigour. He was hoping that life aboard would prove therapeutic. 'Clearly,' he writes, 'I get old. (He was 56.) I never used to get tired and don't like doing it now. My tummy is not very good and I am just looking to the rest on the voyage. If I am not better by the time I land, I will be disappointed. I suppose I ought to treat myself as an invalid for a bit but it isn't easy to come to that yet.'

In letters to Bella Walker, Charles reports that, despite 'a rough cold crossing of the Bay' (of Biscay) where he escaped the sea-sickness that afflicted 'nearly everyone', he 'had a good voyage – picked up a lot in the last week.' Reflecting on his time in the capital, he declares, 'I wouldn't like to live in London in that eternal infernal rush for trains.'

On disembarking, he spent two days at the Cape before making his way north. He was fortunate in getting a "hut" at the Country Club some five miles out of Pretoria and 'quite close to our house (which is) being well looked after as well as the livestock and in spite of the drooth, Edith's garden (is) in quite fair shape.'

He returned to Cape Town on March 23 to attend the Parliamentary Session and was 'quite lucky' to find accommodation at the Civil Service Club, the town being rather full His sister was also residing there temporarily, her house unavailable until the end of the month. As for his in-laws, resident at the Cape, the news is disquieting. 'The Rogers family,' writes Charles, 'are having a bad time. Another of the girls (a sister of Edith's) has had a serious operation since I returned and now the old lady (mother of Edith) is in a Nursing Home after an operation for cataract.'

Almost as a footnote to the letter, Charles casually lets slip an item of news that would gladden the hearts of his many admirers and particularly that of his father. 'Have a letter from the University (of Aberdeen) this mail offering me an LLD. It was cabled to the papers some weeks ago but of course I knew nothing of it. It is mighty decent of them.'

Charles was, understandably, unable to attend the spring graduation which took place in the Mitchell Hall, Marischal College, on 24 March 1920. He was one of three recipients whose degrees of Doctor of Laws were conferred in their absence. Covering the ceremony, *The Aberdeen Daily Journal* of 25 March reported that mention of the name 'Hamewith' – already attached to writer as to writings – "was received with a prolonged cheer" from the assembled undergraduates.

In supporting his candidature, Professor A Mackenzie Stuart, Dean of the Faculty of Law, advanced the following grounds:

Charles Murray, poet, author of "Hamewith" and other works. From a homely dialect he has won rare music: with the poet's vision, he has revealed to us the beauty of familiar things; and he has found a sure place in the affections of all those who know Buchan and its people. For the pleasure he has given to so many readers, for the service he has rendered to literature, and for the treasures he has added to the storehouse of Scottish poetry we ask you to confer on him the degree of Doctor of Laws. To our regret, his absence in South Africa deprives us of the opportunity of giving him personal welcome, and we request that the degree should be conferred *in absentia*.

CHAPTER 13

Twenty-five Years On

'It hasn't been all bad, has it?'
Letter to Edith Murray, 15 July 1920

The months following his return from leave saw Charles caught up in parliamentary business. In the letter to Bella Walker mentioning his LLD offer, he gives a brief insight into departmental/ministerial dealings. 'I have Additional Estimates before the House this afternoon,' he writes, 'and should be there to prompt my minister but he takes so little interest in the Department that I am going to leave him to worry through himself. If he gets into trouble, it may make him give more time to us.'

A few weeks later we are given a glimpse of relations within the Public Works Department. Charles refers to J A Macphail, his former Chief Clerk who had just been promoted to Under Secretary and was ulti-

Charles Murray with Public Service colleagues, John A Macphail (left)
who succeeded him as Secretary for Public Works,
and John J I Middleton, Treasury Department

mately to succeed Charles as Secretary. Of him Charles says, 'He is a very quiet chap but one of the very best; he really runs my Department. I just bluff Parliament and the Public, a branch of the work he is too modest and retiring for. We have sat in adjoining rooms with the door open between us for 15 years or more without a cross word between us which says much for his forbearance.'

In July he is again in Cape Town from where he acknowledges a letter of 4th June from Bella Walker: '... of late I have not felt like writing. Now the weather is better – a dry spell with lovely days though still chilly nights. I don't carry out any of the Doctor's instructions I'm afraid... I suppose I ought really to be put under a keeper but, Lord, life is a poor affair if everything is ordered by rule. I often go to bed seedy and have a bad night but I always get up cheery. I think what I really want is a spring and summer in Scotland. It almost makes me weep; it certainly makes me swear when I hear of Edith sailing on Loch Lomond and I think of all these places I have never seen. Probably I never shall see them unless I look down on them – perhaps I will give my birslin' neck a crick looking up, who knows!'

Presently he reverts to Government affairs. 'I had quite a lively day yesterday,' he recalls. 'First gave evidence before a Parliamentary Committee on Pensions when two of the members had a very hot squabble. Then attended a Cabinet meeting where I carried a point against my own Minister. I rather brushed him aside at the meeting and later in the day I had the cheek to congratulate him on getting the Cabinet to agree, as if he had been in favour of it and he grinned and swallowed it.

'I am now worrying about a Mint we have to erect in Pretoria and will have to send one of my men to London to arrange for machinery etc. It is to cost over £200,000. It looks as if we would be down here (Cape Town) for another month at least.'

Charles did not exaggerate: a month later he was still in Cape Town. His letter of 5 August to George Walker, written while waiting for his business to come before Parliament, focuses on matters personal rather than political. That very day he had stood in for father of the bride when Clive Rogers, one of Edith's five brothers, was married.

The previous Saturday, 31 July, a company of friends, chaired by Sir Caruthers Beattie, Principal of the Cape University, had taken him out to dinner at the Civil Service Club, Cape Town. The event was a double celebration. It expressed the group's pleasure at the conferral on Charles of the LLD; and it extended congratulations on the occasion of the Murrays' Silver Wedding. Regrettably, the pair could not be together on this special anniversary except in thought, for Edith was still six thousand miles away in the United Kingdom. In a poignant letter to her, Charles surveys the landscape of their lives, now sunlit, now shadowed:

DINNER

TO

CHARLES MURRAY, LL.D.
(HAMEWITH)

Saturday, 31st July, 1920
CIVIL SERVICE CLUB, CAPE TOWN

Hot youth is ever a ranger,
  New scenes ever its desire,
Cauld Eild doubtfu' o' the stranger
  Thinks but o' haudin in the fire.
Midway, the wanderer is weary,
  Fain he'd be turnin' in his prime
Hamewith the road that's never dreary
  Back where his heart is a' the time.

Caricaturist's Gift

Office of the Minister of Public Works

Cape Town

15 July 1920

My Dear Wife,

A quarter of a century ago I would have said 'young' wife but we can't be quite young now, can we, no matter how much we might like to be. When your father had his silver wedding, we looked on him as quite an old man, or at least I fancy I did. Twenty-five years looked such a long time to look forward to and now it is past it isn't much. How would we split the time up? The short time in the little first house in Doornfontein; then the spell at Florida which was perhaps the most care-free and happy time of all, only we should have had all three of the children to join us in the evening walk with the dog and the cats. Then the Krugersdorp time which was a bit worrying. Then the first visit home and leaving you and Bill and Peg behind and during the war there was all the anxiety of not having a billet when it finished and at last the relief of getting one. Then the first time living in Pretoria and after that a very pleasant time in our own house in Johannesburg – that was a good spell.

Then you went home and I had a busy while in Pretoria alone and when you came back we had another fine few years in the Sunnyside house and for the last ten years we have had more moving about than we wanted and now this separation.

What will the next bit be – a few more years with the anxieties of retirement to worry about and the education and settlement of the children? And then I wonder if there will be a few pleasant years still left to live in peace and quietness tho' probably still worried about money.

Well, my dear, what do you think of it all? It hasn't been all bad, has it? We have managed to get a good deal of pleasure out of our time in spite of always being hard up. When I look back on my early days as a village boy with patched clothes and bare legs, I have to say I have had lots of good luck to have come so far without absolute failure. I have been in most things fortunate beyond any deserts. As a youngster I always wanted to get a wife who was a lot better in every way than myself, of finer instincts, better breeding and education, and I was lucky in that, and we might have had plain, clumsy, uninteresting children and we have been lucky there. We have always had nice friends and lots of pleasant acquaintances, and I have done a little for my own country and my countrymen have been very generous in their appreciation, and in this connection there is one thing I have always felt grateful to you for – that is the way you put up with my Scots leanings and hobby, the way you entered into them and, instead of just barely tolerating them, got interested when you might have quite reasonably got bored with it all.

Yes, my wife, 25 years ago was a lucky date for me and I suppose in some ways – perhaps most ways – you have not regretted it. A girl takes big risks and she does not realize at the time how big, but we have got through up to now not badly, have we not? One other thing I am grateful for is the way you have treated my relations and friends and particularly my old father. I would have felt it badly if you had looked down on him but you have always been so good to him and have brought up the children to be nice to him too.'

That honest appraisal of their life together rests upon secure foundations: the gratitude, truth and constancy of a devoted man. Love poems are few in the Murray canon, but Charles was capable of touching tenderness and delicacy – as here in *The Hills an' Her.*

> Her an' the hills, wi' me to share,
> An' Heaven itsel' micht weel be there.
>
> A bower o' birks, – O happy dream! –
> A wee hoose happit ower wi' breem,
> A window to the Wast, a neuk
> Weel-cushioned by the fire, a beuk
> O' sangs – the sangs I canna sing,
> For aye as throu' my hairt they ring
> I lift my heid, an' lose the line,
> To meet the een that's waitin' mine

Edith's continuing absence is underscored by Charles's confession in a letter to George Walker: 'I discovered today I had been wearing a coat

to the office for a week all worn out at the elbows – I am not very observant about clothes or particular – luckily I have so far evaded the Prince
(Prince Arthur of Connaught, currently Governor-General). I will be in
trouble as I have never signed his visitors' book and the official dinners
have started.'

In the letter making this admission, Charles is able to tell George: 'I
have a few advance copies of the new book this mail.' The "new book"
was *In the Country Places*, dedicated to 'G.W.S.W. and I.W.' (George
Walker Smith Walker and Isabella Walker) and making its appearance

George W S Walker, life-long friend of Charles Murray and guardian of
Murray family interests

much later than anticipated. 'Seeing it has the initials of you and Bella,' Charles continues, 'I am just sorry it is not bigger and better but such as it is, it gave me very great pleasure to put your initials there and I hope it will give you a little to have it. It is just a straw to show the wind of gratitude that must ever blow from the Murray family to yours.' Then up speaks the meticulous craftsman: 'So far, I notice only three misprints ("compositor's errors" would be more accurate) but they are rotten ones and make nonsense of the words.'

Isabella Walker, wife of George Walker
and companion in care for the Murrays

Before bringing his letter to a close, Charles touches again on the woes of a civil servant: 'Just at present I have no minister as the proper one is ill and the acting is on leave. We are rather in a hole financially as we have spent all our money on some votes and can't get more till Parliament meets in March. So, when urgent things crop up, I will have to exceed and stand the racket of the Accounts Committee. The Treasurer has called a meeting of all Accounting Officers tomorrow, I expect to rub in the need for economy.'

For the most part, in his dealings with others and in his verse, Charles gives the impression of a man of great inner strength and philosophic mind, irradiated with a sense of humour, that kept him from taking himself and his fellows too seriously, rejoicing in the beauty and diversity of life, aware of – but not affrighted by – his own mortality. In the opening weeks of 1921, however, a number of concurrent factors brought his spirits low.

First, his wife, understandably reluctant to bid farewell to their two elder children, had not yet rejoined him from UK. Then, of his three companions on the 1891 trek from Rhodesia – "big powerful men" – one was already dead, a second was dying of heart trouble, and the third, his cousin Jack, was in a mental hospital. On the political scene, uncertainty – bred by pending election results – was unsettling. Discontent was rife in a Civil Service seeking unaffordable salary increases and fearful of retrenchment. 'All these upheavals,' claims Charles, 'reconcile a man to age and approaching dissolution. You begin to feel glad you are nearly through the struggle.' As if the foregoing were not enough, he adds: 'I had my first bad night last night for long, the result of taking a whisky and milk before bed. I suppose I will learn sense some day. However,' he concludes, 'I am fit again today.'

Before February was out Charles was back in Cape Town, accommodated in a very comfortable but expensive seaside hotel, waiting to learn who his new Government minister was to be. The long-anticipated arrival from UK of his wife and younger daughter on board *The Ulysses*, delayed some hours by headwinds, happened to coincide with the opening of Parliament, an occasion that Charles "never" attended. He was thus able to meet Edith and Jean, and assist them through Customs.

Their elder daughter, Edythe Margaret, was in the third year of a four-year Arts degree course at St Andrews University. William, their son, had begun an apprenticeship in electrical engineering at Preston. How best to finance them throughout their studies was a matter currently engrossing Charles's attention.

Reverting to the political front, Charles reports: 'I am now being badgered by MPs who want buildings in their districts and we are feeling the war at last and have no money. We will have a few lean years now.' So far as the ministerial appointment was concerned, however, there was cause for qualified relief: 'I have got the same minister again – not the rotter I had for a bit of last year – but a Scot I have had for the past seven years; only he doesn't take much interest in my show as there is no politics in it.'

Charles had arrived in Cape Town about 27 February 1921, to be on hand for the start of parliamentary business. Towards the end of March he was optimistic enough to predict: '... the session should be a short one... I will be glad when we get back to our own house. I get too old to enjoy living in clubs and hotels.' April came and went, however, and by May 10 he was complaining: 'The session drags on and it looks as if we won't get north before the end of next month.'

What made his protracted bondage all the more galling was his wife's liberty to engage in enjoyable pursuits – not that these appealed to him. 'Edith is having the time of her life,' he grumbles, 'in the sea every day though it is a bit cold now. I haven't been in the sea for over 20 years: it chills me to the bone. I have hot sea-water baths at the hotel in the evening which goes better with my thin blood. She is going to a Government House garden party today. I took care to leave my lum hat in Pretoria, so I shouldn't be dragged out to these social functions.' In a letter of the same period in similar vein, he writes to his son: 'Mother is... living in a comfortable hotel with nothing to do but bathe and mend the tobacco holes in my clothes.' By July he was able to report to George Walker: 'I am just clearing up to get back home (i.e. Pretoria) and am in a rush. Glad to get away from the wet and cold to a decent climate.' He could, however, rejoice: 'Have just got our Estimates passed for another year.'

Charles's health had again been giving cause for concern. 'I think I am a little better,' he writes, 'and am living a very quiet life but I never am *quite* all right, have uncomfortable nights and I suppose one of these days I will let the Doctors have a look inside.'

This may in part account for his idle pen. 'I never write now and seem to have little time to read,' he laments, but he does offer another explanation: 'I can't judge the comparative merits of my own stuff,' (i.e. writing) '… and I am always keen to get folks to pick holes in (it)… one reason I don't do more is that I have no one here to ask for criticism.'

The date of this letter – 21 April 1921 – happened to coincide with a special occasion which prompted further self-revelation. 'This is Edith's birthday, her 50th though she doesn't quite like to think she is as old as that. I am taking her to dinner and a concert tonight. There is a very fine orchestra in Cape Town, all professional. It is a Wagner programme which won't be very enjoyable to me. I wish I had been musical. I'm sure I miss a lot in not being' – self-deprecation that is contradicted time after time in his melodious verse.

Not until mid-September, back in the more congenial surroundings of Pretoria, does Charles speak of having resumed golf – and versifying. 'Feeling energetic enough to have started on one of Horace's *Odes*,' he continues, 'and after two years lying absolutely fallow I find it quite amusing to fit and file words again, but I still find I haven't an idea for anything original left.'

September, the month of his birth, prompted thoughts of retirement, obligatory when he reached the age of 60, just three years off. Despite anxiety over the reduction in income this entailed, particularly with the education of his younger daughter in mind, he admits, 'I find myself planning three years ahead and it generally resolves itself into a spring in Scotland to smell the birks and hear the mavis again.'

Writing to George Walker on the eve of St Andrew's Day 1921, Charles reports: 'There is a banquet in town but I am not going in. I have plenty this week: a State dinner with the Prince (i.e. Prince Arthur of Connaught, the Governor-General) on Thursday; and another on Friday with the Prime Minister. They are farewell functions to the Imperial Officers who are now handing over the defence of South Africa to ourselves.' Then follows a prediction: 'The next step I expect will be – when the Prince goes – a local man for Governor and so gradually we will get to complete self-government if not actually a republic.'

If he was sometimes critical of his political masters, Charles was no less severe upon himself. His self-assessment was clear-eyed, candid, dispassionate. Writing to Bella Walker, he explains his role: 'My job consists greatly in bringing level judgment to bear on people and proposals, and if I have any qualifications for my billet and I haven't much really, it is that I have fairly good judgment… I never was any good at Maths., or anything else really; just had a certain amount of mother–wit which kept me from making an absolute hash of things, and I have always been a lot better at making others do things than at doing them myself. I always say I wouldn't employ myself in my own Department but I have always managed to keep my Chief from finding out what a humbug I really was, so you see, Bella, I have quite a level-headed idea of my own abilities and quite recognise the luck I have had in life. My greatest weakness is incredible laziness… '

His superiors in government clearly did not subscribe to Charles's modest assessment of his own ability. Upon the advocacy of Prime Minister Jan Christiaan Smuts, the name of Charles Murray was lodged for inclusion in the New Year's Honours List of 1922. The proposal was obviously endorsed and in due course its further progress was advised in a brief but cordial communication of December 24 (1921) addressed to "Charles Murray, Esq., C.M.G., LL.D." from the Colonial Office, Downing Street, S.W.1. It read:

> Dear Sir,
>   I submitted your name to the King for a C.M.G. with great pleasure.
>   May I congratulate you on this recognition of your services to South Africa
> Yours faithfully,

The signature was that of the Colonial Secretary – W.S. Churchill.

This recommendation having found royal favour, London Gazette No. 32563 of 31st December 1921, published the citation, couched in the following terms:

> The King has been graciously pleased to give directions for the following promotions in, and appointments to, the Most Distinguished Order of St Michael and St George:-
>   To be Ordinary Members of the Third Class, or Companions of the said Most Distinguished Order:-
>   Charles Murray, Esq., LL.D., Secretary for Public Works for the Union of South Africa.

Typically, Charles regarded the honour not as a personal accolade, rather as a tribute to the entire Public Works Department which rarely gained recognition. He knew it would give pleasure to his father and on that account also drew satisfaction from it.

In the course of a letter to George Walker, written on 11 January 1922, he casually refers to the award: 'Perhaps you saw I had got a CMG. Someone asked me what it meant. I explained it was a sort of new Trinity – Charles, Michael and George. "Colonial-Made Gentleman" is another reading. I was surprised that Smuts recommended me for it as I have never been a Government supporter and I never play up to Ministers – don't even call on my own… years ago it would have seemed worth having I expect but now… One amusing thing about it is I will now be prayed for by name once a year in one of the Chapels at St Paul's. I can imagine the powers above saying "Who the blazes is he? Never heard of him before."'

Such a jesting reaction is typical of one as impatient of formal religious observances as Charles. It emerges in a number of his poems where death is viewed not as an appalling prospect but as an expected, even welcome translation to a sphere where inevitably dues have to be paid, but justice and peace are assured. The spiritual plane is represented in humorously material terms. Witness *The Antiquary*:

> He lived till ninety, an' this deein' wiss
>   He whispered, jist afore his spirit flew –
> "Gweed grant that even in the land o' bliss
>   I'll get a bield whaur some things arena new."

Or the city-slave, robbed of his country idyll:

> The banker swore 'mid siccan scenes to die,
>   "Back to the land" was daily his refrain;
> A fortnicht syne he laid his ledgers by,
>   The nicht he's castin' his accounts again!

Or the farmer with the ultra-pious wife:

> 'Twould only be waste pittin' wings upo' me,
>   Sae short i' the breath an' sae brosy an' big,

For tho' I could reest I'm ower heavy to flee,
  The wife can hae feathers, but I'm for a gig.

A grace to the kail, an' the readin' at nicht,
  Wi', or I gang forrit, a preachin' or twa,
I'll lippen to that when some gloamin' the vricht
  Screws doon the kist lid an' I'm throu' wi' it a'

While Charles could never be termed, in the old phrase, "kirk greedy", nevertheless his poems and letters testify to a belief in God; in the Creator of a world of natural beauty and human potential for good – or for ill; in a just and righteous Judge; and in a hereafter where the spirit dwells. The poet rejoiced in God's "braw birlin' Earth" and recreated it in his verses. From his pen came also a gallery of closely observed characters, but he left the reader to analyse motives and draw conclusions. His own compassion, his readiness to make allowances are nowhere more manifest than in his poem *Still, Man, Still* which ends:

When ye uphaud or I misca'
  There's aye the tither side,
An' whiles the very best o' us
  Would some things hide;
We're maistly a' a mixture, man,
  Like pasture on the hill,
Whaur tufts o' girse an' scrogs o' brecm
  Raise stoot tups still.

The poet portrayed; he did not pillory. Judgment was God's prerogative and judgment was inescapable. In a letter to Bella Walker, Charles makes reference to her children's school examinations before ending on a moralising note: '… one of the good things about old age' – he was then 56 – 'is that there are no exams., though I suppose we ought to be preparing for the big exam. in the next world.'

He makes a similar point in the opening verse of *The Lawin'*:

The way o' transgressors is hard;
  There cometh a day
The Wicked will get their reward,
  The Devil his pay.

And again in that most atmospheric of poems, *A Green Yule*:

> Earth to earth, an' dust to dust, an' the sowl gangs back to God:
>   An' few there be who think their day is lang;
> Yet here I'm weary waitin', till the Master gies the nod,
>   To tak' the gait I've seen sae mony gang.
> I fear whiles He's forgotten on His eildit gard'ner here,
>   But ae day He'll remember me, an' then
> My birn o' sins afore Him I'll spread on the Judgment fleer,
>   Syne wait until the angel says "Come ben."

CHAPTER 14

Conflicts of Loyalties

'There's braver mountains ower the sea,
An' fairer haughs I've kent, but still
The Vale o' Alford! Bennachie!
Yon is the Howe, an' this the Hill!'

Bennachie

The inclusion of Charles Murray in the New Year's Honours List for 1922 occasioned shoals of letters of congratulation. Typical is that of Viscount Gladstone, first Governor-General of the Union of South Africa:

> 21 Abingdon Street
> LONDON, S.W.1
> 2 March '22

My dear Murray

My wife and I were delighted to see your name in the Honours List and we now send our heartiest congratulations. Your public service has been long and admirable and the recognition of it gives us true pleasure.

With all good wishes
Very sincerely yours
H.J. Gladstone

Charles himself, with the deprecation characteristic of the North-east, commented: 'Others seem to think much more of it than I do. I thought more of the LL.D.' Nor was he in any great haste to receive the insignia of this royal recognition. Other matters, both national and personal, were currently of more concern.

'Here we are in for big trouble now, I fear,' he writes. 'A general strike has been declared on the Rand and if it is not settled at once the country will be set back for years. If the mines once start repatriating the natives – and they can't afford to keep them on doing nothing – it will take months and months to get them back and some of the low grade mines will never restart.'

Two months later, from Cape Town where he was attending the parliamentary session, prorogued as a result of the strike, he further reports: 'We are living in stirring times here or, rather, up north. Red Revolution and lots of killing. However it is scotched now and we have to face the aftermath, financial and other. This is the first bit of trouble I have been out of in the last 30 years and I was sorry to miss it. Five times I have turned out with a rifle and I would have liked to make the half dozen.'

Denied an outlet for his martial zeal, Charles had also, it seems, reached a barren spell in his poetic creativity. His most recent volume, *In the Country Places*, had appeared in 1920. Now his publishers, Constable and Co., had raised the possibility of producing the "Collected Works", incorporating all three of his titles. Charles favoured 'postponing a collected edition,' adding: 'I fear, though, I will never have much to add to it. Get terribly lazy these days and, bar some odd Greek translations of the *Epigrams*, have done nothing for years.' He felt guilt at the industry of his admired classical mentor, Sir William Marris, who had sent him translations of over 1000 *Epigrams* and had, moreover, a verse translation of Catullus due for publication.

A little later Charles states his belief that *In the Country Places* marks an improvement on *Hamewith*. He reveals that, to date, sales of his works have exceeded 34,400 copies. By the year's end this had risen to over 35,200. This is a remarkable achievement, an indication of their continuing appeal: '... a mighty lot better than one could ever have dreamed of,' Charles comments, '... not a bad result of what is after all a hobby,' especially, it might be added, for volumes of verse written in dialect. '... now that I have no inclination to write more,' he concludes, 'I feel sorry my natural laziness resulted in such a poor output.'

Early in May, 1922, while still in Cape Town, Charles received from the Secretary to the Governor-General the following communication:

Sir,

I have the honour to inform you that His Royal Highness the Governor-General proposes to hold an Investiture at Government House, Cape Town, on Tuesday, the 23rd May at 12 noon.

I should be glad to learn whether you can make it convenient to attend on this occasion to receive your Insignia as a Companion of the Most Distinguished Order of St. Michael and St George.

Clearly, as his subsequent communiqué to George Walker indicates, Charles had no wish to "make it convenient to attend". In typically casual fashion, he writes: 'Had a letter wanting me to go and be invested with the C.M.G. on the 23rd, but I have no black garments and anyhow won't likely be here. I have suggested to the Prince's Secretary that he drop the cross into my office when passing. He says he doesn't think the Prince will agree but suggests a private investiture. I want to avoid the whole thing if possible. These shows have no appeal to me.'

Nor *did* Charles attend, not, that is, until a later investiture arranged for noon on Monday, the 6th November, at Government House, Pretoria. To personal obligations, however, he was much more responsive, as the following demonstrates.

In July 1922 Charles seized an opportunity to make a token repayment towards a long-standing debt. Writing to George Walker on 8 August, he explains: 'A young Aberdonian, Nan Shepherd, came out on a holiday recently. I met her at the boat and we kept her to see the Cape for a couple of days… Her parents were so good to me in the Cults days it is a pleasure to be able to show her some small attention.' The hospitable kindness of the Shepherd family towards the youthful apprentice was something that Charles fondly recalled even after the passage of some 40 years. Nan Shepherd, poet, novelist, academic, contributed to the 1969 posthumous collection, *Charles Murray The Last Poems,* a discerning appreciation of the man and his creative gifts.

The letter of 8 August lets slip from this most selfless of men his hankering after a little self-indulgence: '… I wish whiles I could run to a motor here. I get fed up at times having to do 12 miles every day in a bus.' It took him some 15 months, but he had his wish, as he presently reveals in a letter to George Walker: 'Perhaps Peg (his elder daughter) has told you of my buying a motor car. I will sell it when I go to the Cape in January. I only want it for learning. Edith is struggling with it now. I want her to be able to take me to the fishing and fetch me at night when I retire.'

In a letter of the same date addressed to his son, Charles covers similar ground: 'Mother is trying to drive the car but not making much of it so far. I find it is good exercise for one thing.' One wonders if he is referring to having to crank the starting handle repeatedly. 'I have damaged my mudguards quite a bit but nothing worse so far. If things go all right I might be able to run to a cheap 2nd hand car at home in '25. It would be fine driving on your roads, but I much prefer to be driven.'

That was all in the future. For the time being, the South African economy was still in serious trouble, as Edith Murray makes clear in a postscript to a letter of her husband's towards the end of 1922: '… I hope it (the year ahead) will be a more prosperous one for all the poor things who are out of work – things are very bad here and I am so sorry for Charlie having to sack his men – it must be a horrible job.' Both Edith and Charles were known for their compassionate concern. To this, Charles Christie, one of Charles's Public Works Department colleagues, paid tribute in a memoir privately circulated two years after the death of his "Chief". He wrote: 'His abounding but discriminating generosity – Murray had no possessive or collector's instincts – attributable to his ancestry and upbringing among those most generous people, the Aberdonians, would flare up at any time; aided and abetted prodigally by Mrs Murray, the two of them would go to great lengths; whether it was a friend or a cause, time or money or trouble, or all three, didn't matter.'

Economic hardship was the lot, too, of Mrs Andrew Reid, Charles's sister in Kimberley. At the close of 1922, Charles wrote to George Walker: 'I saw my sister on the way back from the Cape. She is also in very low water and I will have to assume some responsibilities there. My sister and I never hit it (off) well but after all I must see her through. Her husband is now almost 75 – too old to get any work and Sarah (lately turned 60) and the girl (presumably their daughter, Mollie) try to keep going by a little teaching and a few fowls.'

Christmas 1922 saw the return to South Africa of the elder of the Murrays' daughters, who had completed ten years of education in the United Kingdom. She was joined in April 1923 by sister Jean, down from Johannesburg to spend the Easter holidays at Cape Town.

Charles found the climate of Cape Town taxing and rejoiced when, his parliamentary duties there discharged, he could return to Pretoria, whence in July 1923 he wrote to George Walker: 'It is very fine to be back in this beautiful place in perfect weather. I have got clear of a rotten "Cape Cold" and am feeling really fit and well though just as lazy as ever. General Smuts tackled me yesterday (over) when I was going to bring out another book and professed to be indignant when I said I had given up for good but there it is, though I make great plans to work when I retire.'

Whether improving health or the General's words had provided the spur, a month later Charles is able to report: '... I am feeling fitter these days than for long and have even begun writing again, but only trying Greek *Epigrams* into Scots and I have come to the conclusion that translation can become a bad habit.' The improvement in his health was maintained, certainly until the end of November, when with the triumph of the reformed addict he proclaims: '... I am feeling particularly fit these weeks. Haven't smoked for two months and I am much better of that, but it is a change when you think I have consumed a pound of tobacco a week for over 30 years, but, Lord, it is sad to have no vices left.'

In a letter of the same date to his son, Charles writes of a forthcoming engagement that would have turned his thoughts homewards where they were increasingly focused: 'This week I go to Johannesburg to St Andrew's Night as a guest and have to reply for "Guests"... The Secretary worried me for a message to wire over the country to other (Caledonian) Societies. I am out of the way of that now and all I managed was:

> 'Our Hielan' herts are tuned an' set,
> An' here the nicht we listen in,
> To catch the toast 'Aul' Scotland yet'
> Syne drink an' lat the fun begin.

'The Chief was very pleased with it and wanted to say it was by me, but I only gave it on condition he did not.'

The broadcasting metaphors of the verse may stem from Bill's recent mention of the opening of Aberdeen's own transmitting station. This certainly alerted Charles to the possible value of a wireless set to his father, now denied through failing sight the pleasure of reading. Although initially tempted to retire and return home right away by the image of his father "all by himself" at *Murrayfield*, he arranged instead for his son to buy a set for his grandfather, as a temporary measure. Charles had concerns also on account of the Rogers family. Early in January 1924, he wrote from Pretoria to give his son the news that grandmother Jane Rogers had died in Cape Town of a stroke. The following month brought word from his own sister, Sarah, that their father – now in his nineties – was, according to Annie, his housekeeper, in need of a nurse. Charles at once asked George Walker to enquire of Joseph Watson, currently Ground Officer of Haughton Estate, how matters stood with Peter Murray, his predecessor, with a view to securing additional help. Any expense incurred Charles would bear. When a nurse *was* engaged, he hoped she would ease matters but observed of his father: '… he won't like being bossed up by *two* women.'

Peter Murray (1834–1926), village carpenter and later Ground Officer, Haughton Estate, Alford, Charles Murray's father, at the side gate of *Murrayfield*, his home in retirement

Murrayfield today
Author's photograph

With less than ten months to his 60th birthday, Charles was keenly anticipating retirement – not that there was any decline in his attentiveness to duty but, as each task in the cycle was completed for the last time, the sense of release became more evident. He had hoped to be gone before the State Visit of the Prince of Wales which would involve him in a great deal of additional work. Charles reports: 'Prince Arthur (the Governor-General, due to demit office by the end of 1923) was pulling my leg the other day about the hell of a time I would have (with) the Prince of Wales. We have a big banquet on the 5th – farewell to Arthur.'

Charles did not, however, escape his share in preparations for the royal visit. From Cape Town he wrote to George Walker: 'We are going to have a busy time when the Prince comes out and I have to arrange decorations all over the country.' Nor did he sidestep onerous parliamentary business. 'I would take it very easy this session,' he admits, 'were it not that I have to bring in a Rating Bill. I hoped to complete my service without having to bring in a bill but no such luck.'

How did Charles Murray regard impending retirement? He viewed it with a mixture of relief, of calm, of satisfaction, of gratitude. 'I look forward,' he wrote, 'to dropping into obscurity with great equanimity and it will be something to have finished my job without coming a cropper. I have been lucky so far and have been specially fortunate in having good loyal men.'

As to how he would spend his superannuated leisure, he makes a proposal to his lawyer friend, George Walker: '... can't you get one of your clients to buy Haughton' – an estate on the fringe of Alford, washed by the waters of the River Don, home to salmon and trout – 'I wish I could buy the fishing.'

Charles even nurtures the hope of early retirement should the forth-coming Government elections result in a new Minister of Public Works who would sack him for not knowing Dutch. His comment: 'It wouldn't be very unpalatable if he does.' In this, however, he was disappointed. The incoming minister was a Tynesider, '... the dead image of Charlie Chaplin. I knew him in Parliament and think we will get on all right though I don't care as I am on my last three months now.'

At the handover of ministerial powers, Charles allows himself a note of sentiment, touched with humour, remarking: 'It was rather sad when Smuts' – the outgoing premier – 'had us all in his room to introduce us to our new chiefs; reminded me of a Scots funeral without the biscuit and whisky.' Smuts himself was heavily defeated in the election, but Charles found him 'very philosophic about it and cheerful.'

As his own career in South Africa drew to a close, Charles was constrained to drop a long cherished plan involving his steadfast friend, George Walker. The two had met as teenagers, Charles being the elder by some three years. From that first encounter, despite subsequent long separations, an enduring comradeship and sustained correspondence developed that resulted ultimately in the marriage of their children, Edythe Margaret and Douglas, and was brought to an end only by the death of George in 1934.

Charles felt deeply indebted to the Walker family: to George, a lawyer, who transacted business on his behalf and tendered advice when asked; and to Bella, his wife, who shared with him the role of surrogate parents to the Murray children while they were in Scotland. It was perhaps with the intention of repaying some of that obligation that Charles spoke of having George join him in South Africa on his retirement in September, 1924. He had visions of taking him on a tour of the country he had come to know and love, and of making their leisurely way home together in the spring of 1925.

It was not to be. As retirement approached, Charles became more conscience-stricken over what he saw as the desertion of his father whom he had not seen for over four years. In a letter to George in late May, he writes: 'I note what you say about my father and have made up my mind to get home as soon as I am free even if I clear out for a few months in Spring. I would always regret it if I just missed him; so probably we will sail about the 3rd October.'

Eagerly as he anticipated return to his native Donside and reunion with his father, Charles was well aware of the drawbacks, climatic and financial, of resuming full time residence in UK. Already he had sought guidance from George on the fiscal implications for a home-coming expatriate and had concluded that, for considerations of health and "wealth", it would be prudent to spend six months of each year abroad. Being subject to South African income-tax, he resented the UK taxman laying claim to a further percentage.

Moreover, he was leaving a land that he had grown to love; to the development of which he had contributed significantly; where he had made innumerable friends who would feel the poorer for his going; the land where he had met his wife-to-be and where two of their children had been born.

On the other hand, his had been a demanding career in a climate some-times benign, sometimes extreme. He had had responsibilities over a vast and diverse domain and, like any public servant, had been subject to the vagaries of successive political masters. Little wonder if he welcomed the removal of the pressures of office and the prospect of liberty to pursue cherished dreams.

CHAPTER 15

Departure into Retirement

"Bonnie Charlie's Gone Awa"
Cape newspaper 10 October 1924

As far back as 1906, just half-way into his self-imposed exile, Charles had in the poem entitled *The Alien* drawn telling contrasts between scenarios from his adopted and his mother-land, sharply critical of the former. Verse three voices longing for golf on "links up North" as opposed to the hazards of a South African course, while in verse one (recoiling from the indiscriminate slaughter by explosive charge of what-ever swam in the waters of Mashonaland) he yearns to ply the angler's art. With the advent of retirement he could resume these sports in fair and gentlemanly fashion.

The most authentic and circumstantial account of his angling expertise appears in the 1943 memoir[1] by his fellow public servant, Charles Christie:

"Murray on a trout-fishing holiday at Weltevreden in the Eastern Transvaal had to be seen to be believed. Gay and lighthearted, he seemed to recover his boyhood, full of fun and small practical jokes and good for any mischief. Burn fishing suited him and at Weltevreden there was lots of it. He could always be depended upon to bring home far more fish than anybody else. He took his fishing very seriously. Meals were matters of no importance. Packets of sandwiches, slipped into his basket in the morning, came back in the evening mixed with fish – he had been too absorbed to smoke, far less eat! He had an uncanny knowledge of the natural history of the waterside. The way of a trout with a fly had few secrets from him. He could catch trout on any fly. With a *March Brown* and a *Zulu* he would take fish when nobody else, with these or Messrs. Hardy's latest 'ferlies', could get a rise. One stormy

---

[1] Charles Christie: *Some memories of Charles Murray and a few of his friends* WALLACH (Pretoria) 1943

147

morning of pouring rain with the river coming down in spate, he went off and returned for luncheon with a very fair creel picked up with a big *Alexandra* in a stream the colour of pea soup. But he knew every trick of the trade. Every pool had for him its own method of approach and its own problems; where the set of the current at a particular corner would attract a fish, which side of a big stone he would be under, how to work the fly in the tail of the rush. Those who decry the wet fly technique should have seen it as practised by Murray; they would have learned something to their advantage. The sophistications of dry fly practice had then no attraction for him but, latterly, he was inclined to look more kindly on the dry fly. In the evening after a hard day on the hill streams, when most of the other members of the party would be comatose, Murray would be full of life and enter into the spirit of any prank. One evening he approached his hostess, and holding out a bandaged finger, asked for assistance in tying thread round it. The lady was full of solicitude – such a pity Mr Murray; your right hand too – and when the job was done, after several grimaces indicative of pain, Murray, who had nothing wrong with his finger, gently withdrew it and turned away, leaving her with the bandage."

That was culled from earlier days. Now, at the close of Charles Murray's overseas service, his colleagues were much exercised about how to mark his departure. It was customary on the retirement of an official from the Public Works Department, as elsewhere, to present a piece of silverware, or some such token of esteem. Charles, however, let it be known that, in the words of his fellow public servant, Charles Christie: "he would accept nothing of the kind; that anyone attempting to arrange such a thing would suffer his severe displeasure."

An ingenious solution to this quandary was found, probably by his right-hand man, J A Macphail, who, aware of his Chief's love of angling, proposed cabling a remittance to the Edinburgh branch of Messrs. Hardy Brothers, suppliers of superlative fishing tackle, to be placed to the credit of Dr Charles Murray, enabling him to make a selection beyond his wildest imaginings. Charles was thus confronted with a *fait accompli*. When he was informed of the transaction, there resulted, to quote Charles Christie: "… some plain speaking about the iniquity of presentations, but nothing approaching a riot, and, finally, there came a letter from Scotland full of appreciation for an equipment which was the joy of his heart and which he had never dreamed of possessing."

His colleagues were not alone in wishing him well. A trade journal, *The South African Builder* of October, 1924, reporting his retirement, carried an account of his career, professional and literary, and covered the occasion at which tribute was paid to Charles by those most indebted to him for the prosperity of their industry. The concluding paragraphs of the report give an indication of the high regard in which Charles was universally held:

> The National Federation of Building Trade Employers in South Africa, on behalf of the Builders of the Union, prepared an address on vellum enclosed in a leather case, which, together with a silver salver suitably inscribed, were presented to Dr Murray at an informal function in Pretoria. Mr. A. Andersen, the President, in making the presentation, eulogised Mr. Murray's services and voiced the Builders' regret at his retirement.
>
> The address read as follows:
>
> To Dr. Charles Murray, C.M.G., LL.D., A.M. Inst. C.E.
> We, the Officers and Members of the National Federation of Building Trade employers in South Africa, representing the Master Builders' Associations of Pretoria, Witwatersrand, Capetown, Port Elizabeth, Durban, East London, Kimberley, Bloemfontein, Kingwilliamstown, Grahamstown, Queenstown, Heidelberg, Pietermaritzburg, Dundee, Potchefstroom and Kroonstadt, desire to place on record our recognition of your valuable services and unfailing courtesy during the twenty years you have occupied the position of Secretary for Public Works in the Union of South Africa, and also desire to express our sincere appreciation of the keen interest you have always displayed in the status and progress of the Building Industry. We deeply regret your retirement and sincerely trust that the future may hold for you many years of well-earned rest and happiness.

Doubtless, as his Public Service career drew to a close, Charles found his thoughts returning to its beginning. He was moved to write to his precursor in the post of Under-Secretary for Public Works, Transvaal,

R N Harvey, currently a high-ranking officer, stationed at British Army HQ Simla, Northern India, letting him know of his imminent retirement and expressing the wish that his deputy, J A Macphail, might succeed him. His wish was granted – but not until 1931.

In his reply, Harvey recalled: "It was in September 1905 that I handed over to you without the least anxiety; rejoiced that I was permitted to have for a successor one who would, I knew, maintain the principles laid down by the original Chief (Colonel G H Fowke), in spite of everyone else; you have done nobly, and more than filled the bill.

I have written to Fowke... and I know in his heart of hearts he is extremely proud of his South African infant born in 1902.

... although you may not like it, I am going to thank you sincerely for all you have done not only to maintain the standard of integrity of the Public Works Department, but chiefly for what you have done in establishing the credit of the Corps of the Royal Engineers, to which the founder of the traditions of the P.W.D., so far as they exist, belonged."

In a handwritten letter, Minister of Public Works Thomas Boydell gave approval for the retirement of Charles Murray on reaching the age of 60, with effect from 28 September, 1924. He expressed genuine regret at his departure and warm appreciation on his own and his predecessors' behalf, declaring, "No Minister could wish for a more able and willing Head of a Department."

The Minister for Defence added his special thanks to Charles for the "excellent services" rendered while Director of Works with the Defence Force during World War 1. He spoke "not only on my own personal behalf but also on behalf of the Government to express our very high sense of appreciation for the able and loyal manner in which you have at all times carried out your responsible duties."

Finally, from the Office of the Prime Minister, Pretoria, there came a letter of appreciation from the Prime Minister himself, J B M Hertzog.

UNION OF SOUTH AFRICA – UNIE VAN ZUID-AFRIKA
Prime Minister's Office,
Kantoor Van De Eerste Minister,
Pretoria.
27th September 1924

Dear Dr. Murray,
    Your Minister informs me that you are on the eve of retirement

from the Service, and although this Government has only been in office a short time, I am well able to judge of the merits of the service you have rendered to the Government of the Union.

Let me say that you leave us with distinct regret, and I trust you will long be spared to enjoy your well earned rest after so many years of duty and responsibility. You will no doubt look back with pleasure on your service as a Member of the Public Service of this country.

With best wishes,
      Believe me,
           Yours very sincerely
              (signed) J.B.M. Hertzog

Dr. Charles Murray C.M.G., LL.D.
Secretary for Public Works,
Union Buildings,
PRETORIA.

As a matter of wide public interest, the South African press reported the departure into retirement of Charles Murray and acknowledged his lengthy and distinguished service. In an editorial headed "A Builder", *The Cape Times* of Friday, 3 October, 1924 (the day of his departure) drew consolation from the belief that he had a return ticket. It continued:

"Throughout his long tenure of office Dr Murray, if he has not been able to satisfy the wishes of all sections of the community, has convinced them of his sincerity, of his sound understanding of the principles upon which the great department he controlled should be administered, and of his unfailing courtesy and readiness to meet, where possible, the views of local communities. Moreover, Dr Murray has set a shining example of devotion to public duty throughout his career. That in itself is a contribution to the building up of South Africa which can scarcely be rated at too high a value, and it is part of the permanent impress which he is leaving upon the country."

The Pretoria News of 4 October, 1924, observed: "Many there are who will miss this quiet-spoken versatile man of the North, with the modest ways and the generous spirit."

Under the caption "Bonnie Charlie's Gone Awa", one of the Cape papers, in its edition of 10 October, recognized in Charles Murray "... not only a greatly efficient and greatly intellectual head of the Public Works Department" but "... a very notable poet... He loves Scotland... yet he is a deep and sincere lover of South Africa: its history and romance and people... Outside his office and those fugitive hours when he wrote his fragments of imperishable verse, he was a natural humorist. He had a true instinct for good fun. 'C.M.' is a name that in all four provinces of South Africa is responsible for a hundred good stories... He has achieved a Civil Service record in one respect – he has served under more ministerial chiefs than any head of a department since Union."

On 25 October the Johannesburg *Star* commented: "It was perhaps characteristic of Charles Murray to have slipped away almost unobserved. He will have landed in Britain by this time."

CHAPTER 16

The Exile Returns

'... to the auld hame across the seas at last'
Scotland Our Mither

When, upon his retirement, Charles and Edith returned to settle in Scotland, it was a foregone conclusion that they would choose Alford. Charles would want to be within easy reach of, if not actually resident in, *Murrayfield*, home of his elderly father; and within sight of scenes cherished since boyhood: the angular profile of his beloved Bennachie; the brow of Gallowhill; the gentle contours of the Howe of Alford; the molten bronze of Don where he could set against the wily trout his skills with the superb new Hardy Brothers' tackle. These were the landscapes which from afar he had recreated in his mind's eye and commemorated in verse:

> But Bennachie! Faith, yon's the hill
> Rugs at the hairt when ye're awa'!

★　　★　　★　　★

> The Vale o' Alford! Bennachie!
> Yon is the Howe, an' this the Hill!

Now the reality had been restored to him and he rejoiced – but temperately. Writing to William Will from Pretoria in February, 1922, Charles had divulged his hopes: 'I plan to see you all again in the Spring of '25 – if I'm spared – and, as the old wife said: "if I'm nae spared, ye winna expect me."' Spring 1925 was approaching and it seemed that no sooner were the Murrays home than circumstances obliged them to head south following a family wedding. Charles was also deeply disappointed that a good friend, Alex Keith, scholar, writer, businessman, farmer, having failed to secure the editorship of the *Aberdeen Journal* newspaper, would be looking for a London post.

Charles reports their own reluctance to leave Alford: 'My wife has been pretty seedy since the wedding and we have to clear up and get away on Friday and, man, how loath we are to leave you can't think. If anything, she is more unwilling to leave this countryside than I am.'

He had come home to find himself a celebrity, beset on all sides by invitations to dine and, invariably, to deliver an address. 'If anyone suggests asking me to any function,' he charges William Will, 'you tell them I am on the point of death. As a matter of fact, I am in rude health and have put on about 10 lbs... Man, I am enjoying every minute of every day. I don't feel the cold and I don't miss the sun and, if folks weren't so kind and hospitable, I would be perfectly happy.' Having declined at least a dozen invitations to dine *and* speak, he admits: 'It seems sometimes rude but I can't help it and anyway, so long as I keep my mouth shut, folks won't discover what a poor thing (my delivery) is.'

Mid-December though it was, Charles was able to recount: 'This has been a lovely sunny day and my wife and I motored over the Suie Hill to Clatt then on to Old Meldrum and home by Monymusk and the Lord's Throat. Another good day was through the Cabrach. I had heard of the Cabrach all my life but never saw it before. I just wish it was summer and I could get a cheap car and potter over Scotland.' The Cabrach is a district no more than 20 miles from Alford. That Charles had never before visited it is an indication of how limited travel was in his boyhood.

Having to fend off well-meant dinner engagements was trial enough, but scarcely a month home and Charles had to confront a more daunting approach. A group of respected friends and admirers, seeking to give public and tangible expression to their regard for one who had through his poetic gifts enriched the literary heritage not only of the North-east of Scotland, but of Doric speakers world-wide, proposed commissioning a portait of him in oils and a bronze bust. The first was to be executed by G Fiddes Watt, the second by Harry S Gamley, both Royal Scottish Academicians.

As early as 20 November 1924, a meeting of interested persons convened and a committee was formed. It comprised many eminent figures – civic, academic, professional, commercial, literary. These included Lord Provost Meff of Aberdeen and three ex-Lord Provosts; the Principal of Aberdeen University; four professors; a handful of businessmen; seven advocates; six practitioners of poetry; and, perhaps most touching when it came to the notice of Charles, his former dominie, Anthony McCreadie. Dr J F Tocher, a school-mate of 50 years ago and more, was appointed Chairman, and Charles's closest friend, George W S Walker, Honorary Secretary and Treasurer.

Already the prospect was troubling Charles. He writes: 'The portrait rather worries me, but I couldn't get out of that without offending some whom I wouldn't offend for anything. Fiddes Watt, or his wife, wants me to sit in London which may rather break into my summer holiday. But what is the use of worrying? I am lazy and content and happy to be home and very few can have been so blessed with good friends.'

The public ceremony was, however, still some months away. Of greater and more immediate moment to Charles was the notion of buying a car. Writing from Alford at the end of March, 1925, he alerts George Walker: 'Keep in mind the possibility of coming to London about the 6th May to motor home with me. We think of getting a *Crossley touring de luxe* at £350; the ordinary cost is £440. It should be a good car and last for years... Why not take some lessons in driving next month? Then you could practise on the way up and see if you think it worth while running it the six months I am away.' This bears out earlier indications that in retirement Charles intended dividing his time equally between residence in Scotland and overseas.

From a series of subsequent letters, undated or with dates in May, 1925, and addressed from *St Ives Hotel*, Lancaster Gate, either to George or Bella Walker, it emerges that Charles, after holidaying in Holland and in France, is in London "sitting" for his portrait. At the same time he is making plans to travel to Manchester to take delivery from the manufacturers of the car he has promised himself, cautioning: 'With a new car you are not supposed to do more than 20 miles an hour for the first 300 miles.'

Edith, meanwhile, has been admitted to the London Fever Hospital, 'having developed a white throat and the test (for diphtheria) positive.' Her recovery was slow and punctuated with setbacks. 'It is d – d dull in London these days,' grumbles Charles.

While in the capital, he had word of the death of John Shepherd, father of Nan and a friend dating back some 40 years to his apprenticeship. 'He was such a fine man,' Charles reflects, 'and was so good to me when I lived at Cults in the old days.'

In a letter to his son on *Forbes Arms Hotel, Alford*, notepaper, undated but from internal evidence belonging probably to mid-1925, Charles, now possessor of a brand-new car, describes his drive back from Manchester where he had collected the vehicle from the manufacturers. It was the practice then for a works employee to accompany the customer, especially a novice. In this instance, although Charles had had some driving experience in South Africa, he could hardly be termed an expert. The works driver took the wheel at the outset, handing over beyond Bolton. Charles made for Preston; thence by the English lakes to overnight at Dumfries.

Next day they headed for Edinburgh, arriving before 11 am. Charles had hoped the opportunity would arise then to sit for Harry Gamley, the sculptor engaged to work on the bust to be presented later that year. Gamley, however, was absent. In the evening Charles was able to join his daughter Peg and her fiancé Douglas Walker for dinner, before taking a trip out to Biggar.

By eight o'clock the following morning, Charles and the young driver were on the road, making for Alford via Stirling, Callander, Lochearnhead, Killin, Loch Tay, Aberfeldy, Kirriemuir, Brechin, Fettercairn, Cairn o' Mount and Torphins. 'Between Dee and Don,' admits Charles, 'we ran out of petrol, but the driver took the wheel and coasted down the hill to the Aberdeen road at Tilliefourie where we got petrol. It was a long beautiful day and I wasn't a bit tired.' Something of the order of 470 miles in two days says a good deal for Charles's stamina at 60.

Next day, joined by the senior Walkers and a Mrs Robertson, Edith and Charles went for a drive 'through the Cabrach to Craigellachie and home by Huntly – a fine run, but a bolt got loose on my clutch gear and I had some trouble changing. It is all right now...' On the morrow Peter Murray, father of Charles, had his turn for a spin, which the 92-year-old apparently enjoyed. A trip into Aberdeen was scheduled for two days later to collect Ruth, sister of Edith, who was herself not fully recovered from her bout of fever. 'The car looks well,' continues Charles, confessing, 'I bent the luggage grid backing, but otherwise no damage yet.'

In the months since their return to Scotland, Charles and Edith had been gradually re-integrating into local activities. One body with which they became associated was the Buchan Field Club, dedicated to fostering interest in places and topics of historical and cultural significance. Their presence at the summer meeting at Peterhead on Wednesday, 12 August 1925, is duly recorded. That this was their first attendance, no doubt at the pressing invitation of staunch friends like Alex Keith, James Tocher and David Rorie, is evident from the remarks of the Chairman, Vice-President the Rev Canon Wilkinson, who extended on behalf of the Club a very cordial welcome.

The Chairman's continuing remarks were reported as follows: "The meeting was made memorable by the presence of a Scottish poet, whose name and fame were known to multitudes, but whose name and fame would be known to multitudes more, long after they had been gathered to the bosom of their forefathers. He suggested that they signalise the occasion by electing Dr Murray an honorary member of the Buchan Club." The reporter records: "The suggestion was unanimously and enthusiastically adopted."

Formal business over, the company repaired to the North Eastern Hotel for tea. A toast was drunk to the Buchan Club and reference made to the sterling service rendered by the Honorary Secretary and Transactions Editor, Dr J F Tocher, erstwhile school-mate of Charles. Dr Tocher brought his response to a close by proposing the health of not one, but two, pre-eminent visitors from South Africa: Charles Murray and an almost exact contemporary and greatly admired friend of his, Old Meldrum-born Alexander Aiken, a distinguished economist and educationist, who played a key role in establishing the University of the Witwatersrand, and merits a biography of his own.

In late autumn, from Alford, Charles writes to his son: 'I wish you could have had a holiday here this summer. We could have done some motoring. I want to see Ross and Sutherlandshire. The car has been a great thing... I haven't had a stick-up or an accident yet. Something has gone wrong with the mileage register and (the) garage man does not care to tackle it. It does not matter much as the "speed" registers all right. It is just a pity that neither you nor the girls (Peggy and Marris) could be here to enjoy the car.' He himself had tried to substitute 'a week's motoring in Ross' for a scheduled 10-day golfing trip to Cruden Bay with three companions, 'but they wouldn't so I must fall in.'

'The fishing,' Charles continues, 'has been poor but you should try these new rods; they are beauties' – a reference to his retirement gift from South African colleagues.

As August gave way to September and September yielded to October,

Charles again voiced misgivings over the portrait presentation ceremony. In a letter to William Will who has declared his intention of attending, he comments: 'But I think you are daft to come up (*sc.* from London) all the same. I'll be glad to see you tho', but just at present I am not a bit happy as I feel beastly nervous about next week.' Events had been set in majestic motion, however, and nothing could derail their progress towards a triumphant conclusion.

Great Scot!—CCXXXVIII.

Lieut.-Col. **CHARLES MURRAY,** *C.M.G., LL.D., A.M.I.C.E.*

Bred up by Aiberdeen awa' whaur Dee and Gaudie run,
An' ripened out in Africa beneath the Transvaal sun,
Yon Doric that he fashions mony a canty tune has played—
Isna this a bonny whistle that the gold mines made?

An affectionate portrayal of Charles Murray through a cartoonist's eyes
Courtesy The Bulletin

CHAPTER 17

Honouring a Distinguished Son

'Just when he thocht to slip awa' at last'
Jeames

Thursday, 29 October 1925, the day that Charles had dreaded, finally dawned. From city and county, from capital and colonies, upwards of 500 well-wishers, the high and the humble, subscribers to the tributes about to be paid, streamed towards Aberdeen Art Gallery that afternoon to take their places in the (James) Murray Room of the lately-opened Gallery extension.

The choice of John Buchan, subsequently Lord Tweedsmuir, to make the presentation was doubly fitting: firstly, because he was himself a noted Scottish poet and author; and second, because he was personally acquainted with Charles Murray from their South Africa days. In the early 1900s Buchan had been assistant private secretary to Lord Milner, the then High Commissioner for South Africa and administrator of the Transvaal and Orange River Colonies. Later, while acting Commissioner of Lands in the Transvaal, Buchan would have had dealings with his fellow-Scot, who was at that time Estates Officer in the Transvaal Public Works Department. In introducing the guest-speaker, Chairman James Tocher made reference to this dual connection, observing that John Buchan and Charles Murray had "many experiences and many interests in common: in particular, a complete command of the vernacular and an intimate knowledge of South Africa."

"I count it a great privilege," avowed John Buchan in opening his speech of presentation, "as well as a pleasure, to be allowed to be here today when this ancient city honours a distinguished son... I think it is fair to say that, until quite recently, Scottish vernacular poetry was not one of the boasts of Aberdeen... But now my friend Charles Murray has arrived to fill the blank, and today this north-east corner of Scotland can boast of possessing the best of modern Scottish *makars*."

Buchan recalled the "story of a man who was once found weeping bitterly on the top of a tramcar in Cape Town. He was asked what was the matter, and he replied, 'I have just landed here, and I'm a Scotsman, and, man, it's an awfu' responsibility.' I do not know if Charles Murray was that man but he has certainly lived up to the responsibility and has assisted in making South Africa what most parts of the British Empire are today – a Scottish dependency."

"I think it is due not only to the gifts with which Providence endowed Charles Murray, I think it is partly due, perhaps, to his long sojourn abroad, that in Scottish literature he seems to me to take the larger view and have the larger vision. Exile not only intensifies a man's love of country, it broadens it... Distance mellows prejudices and gives, perhaps, a juster perspective."

"I have said that I am not going to enlarge upon the merits of Charles Murray's work; they are familiar to all of you, they have long been familiar to the world – their humour, their tenderness, their subtle and beautiful melodies. But there is one quality about his work I would like to emphasize, and that is its catholicity. Like Robert Burns, he produces all the great lines of Scottish tradition – what you may call the cavalier and the covenanting, the domestic as well as the wayfaring, the mundane and the translunary. In one word, Charles Murray gives us the broad Scots."

"The true Scot," continued Buchan, "though he is home-loving, is also far-wandering. He is adventurous, both in the material world and in the world of the spirit. His strength, I think, lies in the fact that he has always a fixed centre, so that if one leg of the compass be in Cochin China, the other remains firm in some corner of his native land. I will tell you a story. A friend of mine, during the War, was once visiting wounded soldiers who had returned from Mesopotamia. She asked one man where he had got his wound. He considered for a moment, and then he said, 'Weel, me'm, it was about twa miles on the Rothiemurchus side o' Baghdad.' I like to find in that saying a parable. We orientate ourselves by what we know and love, and therefore bring the whole world within the homely circle of our comprehension. We define the city of the Caliphs by its relation to Rothiemurchus, and, shall I say, at Rothiemurchus we are always looking outwards towards Baghdad. It is this noble mixture of contraries which I call broad Scots; it is the source of what is great in our literature, of what is worthy and enduring in our life."

Following sustained applause, Buchan proceeded to unveil the painting which he then formally presented in these words: "I have now the very pleasant task of offering, on behalf of the subscribers, to our friend, Dr. Charles Murray, this portrait of himself, as a token of the pride and affection with which he is regarded by his own folk."

The 'loud and prolonged applause' that greeted the ceremony erupted in a standing ovation when the recipient rose to reply. In a speech, utterly characteristic of the man in blending modesty, humour, shrewdness and sincerity, Charles made a plea to retain what was worthily characteristic of Scotland's past in language, customs, buildings, ballads, folk songs and tales, dance, music and drama. He even appealed to contemporary lairds to embark on schemes of re-afforestation on the twin grounds of financial return and the creation of beauty.

Not surprisingly, much of his address is devoted to the topic of vernacular writing. "I am not quite certain," he admits to his captivated audience, "if I stand here as a punishment or a reward for having, during many years in a new country, kept warm my affection for the old, and retained my interest in its simple life, its old-fashioned characters and customs, and its couthy and expressive language."

"The charge, I suppose, is that by writing in the vernacular at a time when that was a less popular pastime" (a significant term) "than it is at present, I did some little thing to keep alive the interest in the vernacular, and helped in some very small way to carry it through lean years to more prosperous days. If this is the charge, then I should be very proud if I were found guilty."

"I am very interested in the dialect and vernacular, but I cannot talk learnedly about it. You will remember in *A Window in Thrums*, Tammas, the humorist, said, 'A body canna be expected to mak' a joke and to see it. That would be doin' twa men's work.' So I think a body cannot be expected to write in the vernacular and talk learnedly about it." The last two sentences were received with laughter.

"I confess," he goes on, "it has always been difficult for me to get up very much enthusiasm over the pedigree of our language – whether it is a real, original language dating from the Tower of Babel, whether it is an offshoot or survival of the Old English, or whether it is merely a hotch-potch of all languages that ever were." (Laughter met this stab at sourcing, but the patent honesty of his next admission drew applause.) "I am interested not from the historical but from the human side."

"Now the vernacular as I knew it as a child has lain warm at my heart ever since, and we have to consider – I hear different views of this – whether it is keeping its place or whether it is losing. If it is losing – sometimes I think it is – it is a matter of concern for us all, and we should consider what we are to do about it."

He cautioned, however, against excavating archaic terms from the pages of a dictionary in an attempt to resurrect the vernacular. "I have seen the suggestion that we should dredge Jamieson and go back to the old writers, bring in a lot of the old words that have gone out of use, and build up our language afresh. I do not believe it will do any good, but it will be much if we can preserve for our children the language as we know or, perhaps, as we knew it. Nor do I think it will do any good to teach it in our schools as a language, but the teachers could do a great deal even if they occasionally used some of our sappy words and pithy phrases in their conversation with the children. I do not mean that they should teach the children the vernacular, but get them to feel that there is nothing to be ashamed of in having a good knowledge of their own home language. I can remember as a boy when talking to the teacher we always felt somewhat shamefaced if we could not express ourselves, or properly make our point, without falling back on the Scots. This should not be. The children should be taught that it is the best thing in every way for a nation to be efficiently bi-lingual." Cries of 'Hear, hear,' punctuated this portion of his address.

"I have been living in a bi-lingual country. In South Africa, Dutch and English are the official languages. But the Dutch which is making headway and is popular and alive is not the High Dutch of Holland, but the simpler Afrikaans – the Taal – which has been spoken on the farms of the veld for generations. That is the language which the South African Dutch people are determined is going to last. They have schools where it is used as the medium of instruction, and although there is practically no literature behind it as yet, that will come. That language is more alive than it has been for long. If this can be the result in Africa, taking this country with its wealth of literary possessions in the vernacular, I think something ought to be done to keep our language alive."

Referring to the acquisition of the painting, Charles disclosed: "In my unsettled life I have never managed to get anything which I could regard as an heirloom, and never became the possessor of anything that seemed to warrant the existence of a fire insurance policy but now, thanks to you, and this splendid gift, I am making a great start. When I look upon this, it brings back memories of weeks in the springtime of an enforced residence in London, when the one bright spot, except for a visit to the *Graphic* offices, to Mr Will and Dr Bulloch, was a walk across the Gardens to the artist's studio. I am grateful to him for the trouble he took in connection with the picture and I am even more grateful for the kindly welcome and hospitality of his charming family."

"When I look at the picture in future years I shall always have a certain amount of discomfort, thinking how little I deserved such a splendid gift, but with that will come the memory of all the good friends who have done this for me. May I quote four lines from a living poet:-

> From quiet homes and first beginning,
>   Out to the undiscovered ends,
> There's nothing worth the wear of winning
>   But laughter and the love of friends.[1]"

"In my life I have had all the usual ups and downs, the worries and troubles which everyone gets, but through it all I have always found great occasion for laughter and, more than anyone I have ever known, I have been blessed with my friends. Now to you, Mr Buchan, to my other friends here, and to those friends who are not here this afternoon but would have been if they could, I can only finish by saying from a full heart, 'Thank you' and again 'Thank you.'" The conclusion of his address brought 'loud applause'.

It fell to the Principal of the University of Aberdeen, the Very Reverend Sir George Adam Smith, to make a presentation to Edith Murray. He first endorsed what John Buchan had said of Charles, before going on to rate the latter's achievement with that of Burns in "developing and articulating (the) tremendously vigorous potentialities" of his shire. The Principal then spoke in praise of the volume of verse entitled *A Sough o' War*. "There was no man from the beginning of the War or throughout it who had a truer conscience of our just cause than Dr. Murray had. His notes were always stirring, and, I think, he did more than any other man in Aberdeenshire or in Scotland to rouse and enlist our men to their duty and to the sense of right in fighting for it."

---

[1]   Hilaire Belloc, *Dedicatory Ode*

"There is another side to his poetry than that, and it is the pathos and the tenderness with which he, perhaps more than any other contemporary poet, has celebrated what the women of Scotland both did and suffered during the War."

Addressing Mrs Murray directly, the Principal continued, "... we have resolved to join you in this hearty tribute that we are paying to your husband tonight. It comes from our hearts and we want to present you, as a memorial of the present memorable occasion, with a replica of the bronze bust of your husband by another distinguished Scot, Mr. H.S. Gamley. Unfortunately the replica is not to hand, and so we have to ask you to receive it in faith and with a certain amount of patience, which no doubt you will be able to do, being as you are in happy possession of the original. Without further word I ask you to accept this as our tribute to you as well as to your great and famous husband."

The bronze bust of Charles Murray, superbly executed by Henry Snell Gamley RSA, is now in the possession of Aberdeen Art Gallery. More than a good likeness, it somehow conveys the *essence* of the man – purposeful, determined, with a hint of humour about the lips. The hair, thick with a tendency to curl, is receding, emphasising the high, broad forehead slightly furrowed. Bushy eyebrows overhang piercing, deep-set but compassionate eyes. Lean features are accentuated by the aquiline nose. An ample moustache conceals somewhat the fullness of the mouth. The ears, if large, are set close to the head; the chin resolute. It is a finely proportioned face, full of character, the gaze direct. As befits a military veteran, the head is held erect, the neck muscular. An open-necked shirt lends an informal air as of the veld.

As her spokesman, Mrs Murray had chosen Robert Niven, a long-standing friend from South Africa. Before concluding his remarks, he sought leave to remind, or indeed inform, his listeners that Charles Murray deserved recognition on grounds other than his poetry.

"In our land he is known as an engineer, as an administrator, as the permanent head of one of the great Departments of State in South Africa. He has served under many forms of government – for we go in for changes occasionally in South Africa. Mr Murray has served under military governments; under a Crown Colony government; under partly representative government; under fully representative government; under responsible government; under Union government; under Dominion government; sometimes under mob government; and very

Bronze bust of Charles Murray, executed by H S Gamley, RSA (1925)
Courtesy City of Aberdeen Art Gallery & Museums Collections

often under no government at all. During the whole time he has carried on the work of his Department without turning to right or left. I can assure you, not from hearsay but from my personal intimate knowledge, that his reputation there stands very high as an able and conscientious administrator, as one whose department was always run just about as perfectly as it could be. Everything was done well and done so conscientiously. He has got a great reputation in South Africa, and what you have done today, believe me, will find an echo in many, many hearts in that country. And when he goes back – as we know he is going, because no man who has lived half his life in that country can ever stay away from it – he will get from his many, many friends there a most hearty welcome."

"I am sure if there is one thing Mrs Murray would have asked me to say, it would be this, that she perhaps regrets thinking of her life with him in the future when just so much has been said about him. Yet if I were to sum up her feelings today, they could be summed up best in a few words of Stevenson's, where he said in another connection, 'She's vexed, but kind o' prood.'"

That evening, at a private dinner in his honour, a toast to the health of Charles was proposed by his friend, Cults physician and poet, Dr. David Rorie, who felt constrained to take metrical wing. He begins:

CHARLES MURRAY

Weel, Chairlie lad, it fa's to me
To tak this job up seriously,
Sae here's the metre wi' a canter
That served a' richt for 'Tam o' Shanter,'
Tho' in my han's it's mebbe mair
Liker a tub row'd doon a stair;
But still, aneth your very nose,
I daurna gie your health in prose.

One hundred and ninety-one whimsical, witty and, at times, ironical lines later, Rorie delivers the charge:

Far hae I wandered, muckle said,
As ae thing to anither led,
But a' throughout I hae exprest

Due admiration for oor guest,
Sae, fill an' rise – noo, dinna hurry –
(Ye've plenty time!) Here's 'Charlie Murray!'

CHAPTER 18

Fathers and Sons

'Some threep the moral's this, "Ye'll ging never sair amiss
Gin ye hearken wi' a ready lug when aulder fouks advise."'
The Three Craws

A few days after the presentation ceremony, Charles and Edith arrived
in Rome at the start of what was to be an annual six-months sojourn
abroad to escape the chill of an Alford winter and the harsh exactions of
the British taxman. The passage of time did nothing to remedy matters.
Writing some years later to George Walker, Charles notes: 'I see the
income tax has been raised at home making it more difficult than ever
for us to settle there. I doubt whether it is worth £400 or £500 a year
for the privilege of living in Scotland much as I love it – and I funk the
winters.' Rome had been chosen as their first haven, Charles explains:
'… principally because an old pal goes there every year and would put
us up to the ropes.'

In his first letter to William Will from *Pension Suez, 55 Via Francesco
Crispi*, he gives an amusing account of his early impressions: 'We had a
pleasant journey and once we got on to the train at Boulogne we had
not to get out until we got to Rome next night. We were met by an old
Aberdeen friend and taken to the *pension* where he lives. It is quite
comfortable, in the English quarter and cheap – a double room with two
dressing-rooms and a covered-in verandah and we pay about 7/- each
per day… not a swagger place but good enough for us and, if we don't
like any meal, they are always ready to give us fresh eggs.'

'Rome is full of interest and still more full of priests. We meet them
in hundreds as they are the chief industry here. All nationalities – Chinese
and Irish, Canadian and African and in all stages of manufacture: shaven
and bearded, with shoes and without, some washed, many not. Every
second house is a church or a monastery or nunnery and in the houses
between they sell rosaries and Virgins. You get tired of eternal Virgins
in churches and shop windows and on street corners; and it was almost
a relief to be accosted one afternoon by a lady who evidently had not

been a virgin for many years.'

'We think of staying here for four months or so and then working slowly north with a week or two at Florence, Venice and Milan and then back to Donside and trout fishing by middle of May.'

At some point during their residence in Rome, the Murrays learned that their son was going through a bad patch in his career, being both 'disgruntled and worried over (his) prospects'. In an attempt to cheer and encourage him, Charles wrote at some length, drawing upon his own experience and, incidentally, shedding light upon his career details, his fluctuations of fortune and feeling.

'When I was your age and even older,' Charles begins, (Bill was 28), 'my prospects were not very bright and I used to get down and wonder if I would ever make good. I felt I knew little and wasn't of much use and never likely to be. I was surveyor on a mine and had to measure up for contractors every month, unpleasant work and difficult to do satisfactorily and there did not seem much prospect of getting anything better. For about nine months I worked every Sunday to avoid stopping the working of the shafts and there was no overtime or extra pay.

Once, when in hospital with some sort of fever, I got crazed a bit as patients often do when feverish and I got it into my head I had got another billet and hadn't to return to the mine and it was not a pleasant awakening when my head cleared and I realized I had to return to the old job.

Later on, when the Florida mine closed down and I was out of a billet for a time, things again looked gloomy as they did during the Boer War when I had no job to go to at the end. Even in the Government service there were plenty of anxious times. I never expected to keep my billet long enough to earn pension. I expect the same thing happens to most men and it must be very rarely that men are sure of themselves and confident of the future right along.

The only thing is sit tight, always do your best and wait for opportunities of better things. Once, when older than you, it seemed as if life held little more and I was to be a failure and I remember my sister cheering me up by saying the best of my life was to come yet.'

Writing in much more relaxed vein to George Walker early in February, 1926, Charles muses: 'I hardly know myself here. I even go to Church on occasion and go tea-drinking with wrinkled old spinsters and widows and am generally devilish domesticated.'

In a further letter to George some two months later, still addressed from Rome, Charles indicates their travel plans: 'We will probably start on the homeward journey about the 23rd' (presumably of April)... 'we expect to be in Edinburgh for some days about the second week in May.'

At some point during the Murrays' absence from UK, a group of Charles's closest friends hatched a benign conspiracy. The same swell of admiration and affection for the man that had given rise to the presentation of portrait and bust lay behind the surreptitious creation during his overwintering in Europe of the *Sit Siccar Club*, an informal fellowship in honour of Charles, assembling as whim decreed. Instigated by Dr James Tocher, it numbered among its members Lord Tweedsmuir, Lord

Alex Keith M.A., LLD (1895–1978), friend of Charles Murray from about 1918 until the latter's death, was diversely gifted: journalist, editor of Northeast songs, lover of Doric poetry, farmer, celebrated raconteur, biographer, bibliophile, Keith oversaw publication of the poet's hitherto uncollected verse *The Last Poems* (1969)   *Courtesy Aberdeen Journals Limited*

Boyd Orr, Sir Patrick Duncan, Dr David Rorie, Professor Alexander Gray, Major M V Hay and Alex Keith (who had not after all re-located to London). Possibly the seed had been sown by Charles himself. In a letter written from Rome to Alex Keith, he refers to earlier talk of establishing a fraternity with membership confined to "'those G. (C.M. Grieve) has no use for" but then what a large company we would be, but also what a clubbable crowd.'

The conspirators' choice of name had been the *Hamewith Club*, a suggestion promptly quashed by Charles who proposed the alternative, *The Sit Siccars*, as better befitting a body more comfortable sitting than standing. *Sit Siccar* is the Aberdeenshire term for the securely anchored creeping buttercup. Dr Rorie recommended a limit of 15 members, while Major Hay opined that members were born into the club, not elected; and that rules were taboo – a prohibition that was itself a rule, as Alex Keith observed. In a letter to his close friend William Will, undated but subsequent to the Murrays' move to Banchory, Charles portrays the *Sit Siccar Club* as 'a dozen or so of our cronies who meet at odd times and dine and drink, Tocher and Alex Keith head deisters.'

The club had its own guide on members' conduct – a 16-line poem from the pen of Charles Murray, entitled *Advice to the Sit-Siccars*, which counsels keeping a low profile under stress. Alex Keith implies a link between the *Sit-Siccars* and the earlier *Calm Soughers*, a coterie of Aberdeen doctors that had been in the way of foregathering for weekends at the Kilmarnock Arms Hotel, Cruden Bay. The opening lines of the *Advice to the Sit Siccars*, however:

> Keep aye a calm sough
> An' jouk to the jaw.

incorporate expressions found in Sir Walter Scott's *Rob Roy*. Recalling the genesis of the poem *Margaret Dods*, it is at least possible Charles was re-visiting Scott.

Following their return from Italy in May 1926, Charles and Edith had a welcome visitor at their home close to Alford. This was Ruth, a younger sister of Edith's, one who regarded brother-in-law Charles as an ally and adviser on financial matters. Her enthusiasm for the scenery of the North-east, viewed as she was taken on tour in the Murrays' car,

Portrait (1937, by Alex Christie) of Dr James F Tocher (1841–1945), County
Analyst, Aberdeenshire; from schooldays on, friend of Charles Murray whose
poems *J.F.T.* and *Ae Year's Bairns* were addressed to him.
Courtesy Aberdeenshire Council Arbuthnot Museum, Peterhead

delighted her host who, in a letter to son Bill, himself now at the Cape, voices their regret at her departure for South Africa.

The letter continues: 'We are trying to settle where to go for the winter. Your mother seems to fancy Italy so I expect I will have to fall in.' A subsequent letter to their son indicates that they did indeed go to Italy, but prior to his departure Charles reports to Alex Keith: 'I have been away at Gullane (Lothian) with my old friend Sir W Marris (his former mentor/disciple in classical verse translation in Cape Town 1907—08)... golfed twice a day badly and talked half the night... besides being a big administrator he is a great scholar.'

That autumn Charles had more than golf on his mind. He had consented to Constable, his publisher, bringing out a Collected Edition of the poems previously published in the *Hamewith* of 1909, *A Sough o' War* and *In the Country Places*. Alex Keith very readily agreed to proof-read this new edition. Before submitting the material for reprinting, Charles admitted: 'I felt inclined to try and revise and possibly improve some of my things but I remember... you spoke strongly against any alterations once a thing was finally printed and as this goes well with my natural sweerness (*sic*) I will refrain.'

In due course, the new edition appeared under the title *Hamewith and Other Poems*. It bore the same three dedications as the original volumes and retained the glossary. Introduction and illustrations were, however, dropped.

The Murrays' 1926–27 winter sojourn in Europe had scarcely begun when an urgent summons brought Charles back to Alford from Vevey post-haste: his father was *in extremis*. The race was in vain. Charles reached Aberdeen before noon on Thursday, 11 November, only to learn, as he writes to Bill, that Peter Murray 'had passed away peacefully in the night. He became unconscious on Saturday (6 November 1926) and remained so with no pain till the end... The funeral is on Saturday.'

'I can't feel sorry about grandfather. It is better as it is. I find he was in his 93rd year not 96th as we thought. It is a good age, too long really except in exceptional cases.'

The *Aberdeen Press and Journal* of 12 November 1926 carried a tribute to the "patriarch", which reads in part:

Mr Murray was a devoted employee, strict and upright in all his ways, a skilled tradesman, a keen curler, a good man with rod or gun. He had a number of hobbies, and it is interesting to note that these included the writing of poetry. His rhymes in the vernacular, though they never appeared in print, were very readable, and droll in sentiment. He took great delight in reciting poetry and his famous son undoubtedly owes a good deal to his father's command of the vernacular. He read extensively, and executed a considerable amount of wood-carving and fretwork. Another of his hobbies was the study of geology. He had an excellent collection of geological specimens. Mr Murray was all his life a keen Parish Church man.

From members of the Farquharson family, Peter Murray's erstwhile employers, came letters of condolence to Charles. Miss Anne declared: "No family has been more loyally and faithfully served than ours has been by him – it has always been his first thought and we shall always remember him with true affection and gratitude."

In *her* letter, Miss Elizabeth spoke of the pride Peter Murray had taken in his son's achievements: "... and when he was inclined to be depressed," she continued, "could the subject be turned on to you, his face would light up and he was young and full of spirit again – thinking of what you had been as a boy and all the way up to your success in South Africa.

Dear old man, we must all rejoice that he is at rest and his long wait for the call to cross over is ended, and we must surely feel assured that now he passes to the reward of his faithful, upright, noble life spent so splendidly in this world."

Writing from Bournemouth, a third sister, Miss Maria Sophia assured Charles: "Your father will be remembered always by all those who came in touch with him for his kindness and graciousness of manner – for his great faithfulness to duty throughout his long life."

Before returning to mainland Europe to resume wintering there, Charles seized the opportunity to see Sir William Marris again. To the former's great satisfaction, he was instrumental in having H S Gamley, sculptor of his bronze, execute a bust of Marris to be exhibited in the Chamber of the Legislative Assembly, India, of which the latter was a distinguished member.

Thoughts of his late father might well have occupied Charles while he journeyed back to Vevey. Perhaps he recalled the paternal advice given as he set out to make his way in the world: "Do your best." When it came to offering counsel to his own boy as he embarked on *his* career, Charles could draw upon a wealth of worldly wisdom garnered from a quarter of a century observing and associating with people of rank and authority. Since Bill was currently at the Cape, South Africa, Charles urged him to cultivate the acquaintance of those whom he himself had come to know and respect.

Three months after his brief and unforeseen visit home, Charles wrote from Rapallo on the Gulf of Genoa to his son: 'Now that (the South African) Parliament is sitting, I would like you to call on Patrick Duncan... He was Minister for Interior in Smuts' Government and I saw a lot of him. He is a farmer's son from Banffshire and a good chap, rather dour and silent but his wife makes up. She is very charming... and they have three great boys...

You should go some Sunday afternoon. It is just as well to know these people. You never know when it may come in useful. Anyhow it is always well to get to know interesting people who count. Just tell them who you are and that I told you to call. Don't forget.

By the way, you ought to go up to Government House and write your name in the Visitors' Book... then, when there is a garden party, you will probably get an invite. If you do, look out for the Lady Secretary, Miss Braginton, a thin old thing who will likely be standing alongside the Princess. Look for a chance after the ceremony of receiving to go and speak to her. She is a dear and a great friend of ours and used often to come down to my office and sit and smoke and gossip. If the Lanes are there... they would introduce you and perhaps when a Government House Ball came on she would see you were invited. Don't think it is not worth while. It is and you should not miss any chance of that kind. It is all experience and it always improves your standing among people.'

Among the "interesting people who count", to quote Charles, would have been J J I Middleton of the Department of Finance, Union Buildings, Pretoria, from whom he had had re-assuring news of the discovery of his dispatch box left behind, more than two years previously when he sailed from South Africa upon his retirement. 'This is a great relief,' writes Charles. 'I left the keys with Macphail (a senior colleague) to give to (Middleton) when he got back from leave and it has taken the PWD all this time to discover the box which I left on the floor of my old room and which they at last found exactly where I left it. It had my shares, life policies, etc. and I was quite worried about it.' This oversight suggests a hasty departure from Pretoria to Cape Town where, within a week of his 60th birthday Charles and Edith had embarked for Britain. It reflected, no doubt, his acute anxiety to be reunited with his father, then in his nineties, whom he had not seen for over four and a half years. Now had come, as Charles wrote to George Walker, 'the end of an old song.'

The same letter reflects on the fact that, in the course of the year now nearing its close, the enduring Walker/Murray friendship, born in the early 1880s, had been enriched by the marriage of Douglas Walker and Edythe Margaret Murray. 'When you came out there,' muses Charles, presumably meaning Alford, 'as little more than a boy, we would have thought it a wonderful outcome if we could have foreseen we were to be fellow fathers-in-law. Doug. and Peg. seem to be enjoying life and now it looks as if Bill (the Murrays' son) intends getting off next year.' Bill was indeed married the following year, on 16 March 1928, "at the Cape", if credence may be placed upon snatches of letters from Charles to 'Maggie' (Margaret McCreadie, daughter of his Gallowhill School dominie) and to George Walker.

With the assistance of George Walker, Peter Murray's estate was wound up. To Joseph Watson, his father's successor in the post of Land Steward, Charles wrote expressing thanks 'for all his kindness to the old man...' A long life of good and Godly service had drawn to its tranquil close.

CHAPTER 19

Horizons Old and New

'Wi' a' the warl' to wander,
An' the fine things yet to see,
Will ye kilt your coats an' follow
The lang, lang road wi' me?'

The Tinkler

On retirement, the pattern that Charles adopted was, broadly speaking, to spend winter and spring in Europe, summer and autumn in Scotland. Where exactly Edith and he resided while on "home" ground in Alford is difficult to determine. Since they passed no more than six months in any fiscal year in UK, they chose not to become property owners, preferring to occupy hotel accommodation or lease a house. The hotel favoured was the *Forbes Arms*, Bridge of Alford, delight-

Forbes Arms Hotel, Bridge of Alford, inspiration for *The Brig* and lodging for the Murrays while on leave and prior to moving to *The Lythe*, Banchory
Courtesy Mr Charles Spence

179

fully characterised in the poem entitled *The Brig*, attributed to the late twenties. It opens:

> Twa roads: a corner stane to guide;
>   A puckle trees; a brig;
> Broun water faur the fishers wyde,
>   A gaivel't shop; a gig.
>
> An open door faur roses rin
>   To some Laird's Airms abeen;
> 'Twas weel to win that couthy Inn
>   Ae droothy aifterneen.

Although there appears to be no documentary evidence to support the claim, the Murrays reportedly on occasion resided at *Don Cottage*, a handsome dwelling overlooking the river, close by the *Forbes Arms* and owned by Mr Charles Spence, proprietor also of the hotel. Mr Spence's son, who succeeded to the property, recalls Charles Murray courting Edith's displeasure by hobnobbing with the hotel staff after hours, enjoying oatcakes and milk.

At nearby Montgarrie Mills, the late miller, William MacDonald, who had been personally acquainted with Charles Murray, styled him a hard-headed businessman – literally. As a party-piece, Charles would place some walnuts on the table and bring his head down on them forcibly enough to smash the shells.

Shells of another kind feature in the experience of Mrs Jean Duncan, daughter of Joseph Watson who succeeded Peter Murray, the poet's father, as Ground Officer of the Haughton Estate around the turn of the 19th century. In the front garden of her cottage on Donside Road are large tropical shells, souvenirs that Charles would bring for friends when he came home on leave.

Another long-time Alford resident, Mrs Nan Sandison, daughter of Tom Donald who was shepherd to Captain Cook of Asloun Estate, three miles west of the village, cherishes two memories of Charles Murray, vivid yet across the years. Her first is of being introduced to him when she was a little girl. The year was perhaps 1929; the day was certainly a Sunday, for that was when Charles was in the way of coming to lunch with the captain. Later the pair would go walking on the estate. On the occasion in question, they happened to drop in on *Drumnafunner,* the shepherd's sheiling on the slopes of Langgardlie Hill and it was there that the introduction took place. Nan recalls Charles as a man above average height, with a white moustache. His companion, permanently disabled when a horse fell crushing both his legs, got about with the aid of two walking sticks.

Nan's second recollection is again of a Sunday, this time, however, in a church setting. That Charles Murray was an infrequent church-goer has already been mentioned, but in retirement he did from time to time attend worship. The image that Nan retains is of the Murrays arriving at the West Church barely in time for the start of the service and unprovided with Bibles or hymnals. Someone would hastily furnish these but, noted Nan, fascinated, not a word did the poet sing. Incidentally, she found the minister, the Reverend Robbie Crawford, diverting also. When paying pastoral calls at her home, he would bring "sweeties" for Daisy – the family cow.

'Discourse of the elders': Charles Murray pays heed to his former dominie, Anthony McCreadie (c. 1928)

In 1929 the Murrays' annual "home and away" regime was interrupted. Writing from Alford in August of that year to Maggie McCreadie, his former schoolmaster's daughter, resident now in Aberdeen with her father, Anthony, active still despite advancing years, Charles apologises for his inability to visit: 'Just a line to say "Goodbye". The car is out of action and we are in such a rush packing there is no chance of seeing you, I fear. We sail by the *Ceramic* from Liverpool on the 31st. Will look forward to seeing you both in '31.'

Sadly, it was not to be. Charles and Edith were about to embark upon an extended tour, embracing South Africa, Australia, New Zealand, Japan and Canada, exact duration undetermined. Long before their return, Anthony McCreadie had departed this life. On the morning of Monday, 12 May, 1930, he had as normal played a few holes of golf over the Bieldside course. That evening at his home, 10 Wellbrae Terrace, Aberdeen, he passed away. He was 84 years of age. Charles had earlier remarked on his old dominie's stamina: 'He is 79 and plays golf every day. If he gives the ball as lusty skelps as he used to give me, he ought to get good distance.' He had delivered his last "skelp".

Edith's reaction to their travels is not recorded, but for Charles revisiting South Africa was a heart-warming experience, not least because for a time he had the company of James Tocher. 'It was good to see the Cape again,' wrote Charles to his son, 'and I enjoyed the sun and our run round the Union was most enjoyable, seeing the old scenes and people again. Dr Tocher enjoyed his month. He was keen to meet important people and for the first eight days I introduced him to a Knight a day and wound up with our only South African hereditary Peer – Lord De Villiers.'

To William Will Charles voiced similar sentiments: 'It was good to see the old places and people again and flattering to get such a welcome after five years, from the Governor and his Princess down – we had lunch with him.'

Writing to George Walker from Cape Town on Boxing Day 1929, the eve of their departure for Australia, Charles concedes: 'The rush round the Union with Tocher was a bit strenuous but he saw a lot.' Only on one matter did the pair fall out – Tocher's insistence on keeping a detailed diary which he would lock away in case Charles destroyed it, probably because it chronicled to his companion's discomfiture the pleasure and affection manifest among friends and former colleagues when Charles revisited familiar haunts. Months later this grievance still rankled. In a letter to Alex Keith, Charles upbraids Tocher for his long silence, supposing him 'too busy writing up that d—d diary of his.'

One cloud cast a shadow over Charles's return to South Africa – the death there in his 78th year of Andrew Reid, his brother-in-law, husband of his sister Sarah. 'I was sorry to just miss seeing the old chap,' Charles writes in a letter to George Walker, 'but I fancy his passing was a relief to my sister. She is struggling away with her teaching and I will have to do a bit more for her than I have been doing, I suppose.'

About the passage to Australia, seen as a stepping stone to his true destination – New Zealand, Charles was less than lyrical. 'The voyage… is slow but we had some nice people and none who were objectionable and got some bridge. Several passengers are friends of friends of ours. One, a son of some Lord or other – not He of Hosts – is Chairman of some Australian companies. He placed his office car at our disposal at Perth and we saw the place and the surrounding country in comfort. Spent one night on shore and shared a bed with, I fancy, all the fleas and mosquitos in the Commonwealth. Found an invite there to lunch with the Scots Society at Melbourne and spent the rest of the voyage planning how to evade the ordeal.'

'Perth is a pretty place and Adelaide, our next stop, still finer…' When it came to Melbourne, the press was there to greet the poet. *The* (Melbourne) *Herald* of 23 January 1930, reported: "Yesterday the author arrived in Melbourne by the *Nestor,* and modestly told an interviewer that he regarded his verse-writing as 'youthful indiscretion.' Dismissing this as a "conventional" but not "altogether candid" response, the interviewer, C J Dennis, claimed: "No writer of such verse as Mr Murray's could fail to exult a little at times, privily at least, over an achievement as graceful and patently sincere as it is rare in these graceless days."

'At Melbourne,' Charles resumes, 'an old fellow apprentice in Aberdeen met us with his wife and car… Melbourne is a beautiful city, wonderfully laid out – that was explained by an Inverurie Scot who told me an Elgin man laid it out… '

'I couldn't get out of the Scots lunch but numbers were reduced and I got over it easier than I feared. One of the "head yins" was the Scot from Inverurie. A son of Laing the plumber, he recently retired as General Manager of one of the Australian banks… '

'My friend – also a Laing but from Rosehearty drove us to see his holding which he has named *Hamewith* – he is a cousin to Mrs Fiddes Watt (wife of the artist who executed the poet's portrait). On the way he drove into a snag and threw me against the top of the car. I bled like a pig and had to get a few stitches put in my nose when I got back to Melbourne two days later.'

'We trained to Sydney… too much of a skyscraper American town. This harbour must have been fine when God finished with it but man has managed to spoil it… We met some old friends…' – a regular occurrence.

'A smooth voyage to New Zealand but I am forgetting. At Melbourne we dined with Dr Littlejohn, LLD, of Aberdeen and a big figure in Education both in New Zealand and in Australia where he is head of the Scots College, a great place with 1400 pupils. His father was watchmaker in Alford. I can just remember it. At Sydney I met Dr Wallace, an Aberdonian, Vice Chancellor and Principal of the University. His father was a blacksmith. A good chap, Dr Wallace wanted me to meet the Highland Society but no fear. With considerable trouble and a bit of rudeness, I have evaded reporters rather successfully.'

After a few days in Auckland, their New Zealand landfall, where they 'met an old friend in the Professor of Classics, Paterson,' the Murrays journeyed the 85 or so miles to the base of the Coromandel Peninsula where lies the 'dead mining town' of Thames, the real focus of their visit to the antipodes. Among its dwindling population was an 86-year-old widow in distressing circumstances. Bedridden, paralysed and all but blind, with neither family nor money, she was nevertheless sound of mind and courageous of spirit. On marriage she had become Mrs N Scott, but her maiden name was Robbie: she was a younger sister of Charles's long-dead mother.

'The great thing,' enthused Charles in a letter to his son, 'has been seeing my old aunt and of course that was our main object. It has been so interesting to me to hear about my mother, and what a treat for the old thing to see one of her own people from home after 60 years.'

To Alex Keith Charles confided: '(Aunt) said she was just living to see us. We stayed three weeks and saw her once or twice a day… We had great talks about Birse and Aboyne as you can imagine. A dear old thing, we found it quite difficult to come away but hope to be back in a week or two and find her still alive. I am glad we came, as we were able to fix her up so that she has no financial worry.'

The Murrays travelled extensively in New Zealand, greatly impressed by the country and its people. Of the Maoris, Charles wrote, 'They are a fine race and a sporting. In the old days, when fighting with the whalers one time, they cut a road from the sea to their stronghold so that the invading white men should not be too tired getting through the bush to put up a good fight when they arrived.'

At Lake Taupo Charles saw fishers taking 10 lb trout '… but that sort of fishing,' he remarked, 'does not appeal to me a bit. I want a small stream where you can fish dry fly and I have brought my rods and tackle all this way and never taken them out.'

One of the highlights of their tour was an encounter at Blenheim with a family of second cousins Charles did not know he possessed. They and he shared 'great-grandfather Christie from Torphins… Five boys and a girl and such a fine lot,' exclaims Charles; 'all married with delightful families… It has been such a pleasure meeting these people. They knew of me though I had not heard of them and, as soon as we met, it was just as if we had known each other all our lives.'

Other relatives, hitherto unknown, surfaced in Timaru and in Ythan Street, Invercargill, where roads bear the names of Scottish rivers. The Murrays' hotel there, for further instances, stood at the junction of Dee Street and Don Street. Finding himself later in Christchurch, Charles took the trouble to view the college where his friend, Sir William Marris, spent his early schooldays. At the hotel where Charles and Edith lodged in the city, the landlord was a Turriff man.

Across the country, Charles came upon countless folk with Scottish connections, eager to welcome someone from "home." 'Dunedin is… full of Scots. It is strange to meet people with a Scots accent who were born here. By a lucky accident we found the City Engineer, Alexander, was an Aberdonian who served his time in Walker and Duncan's, (*sic*), starting about a year after I left that office. He and his Aberdeen wife couldn't do enough for us and for three days motored us all over the place. We were sorry to leave.'

Such positive experiences induced in him a pensive mood. Writing to William Will, he reflected, 'More, much more, than ever we realized how full of kind folks the world is. Everywhere we went we met with kindness – from old friends, from new and from strangers. If there is anything in travel, it is that it gives you an appreciation and understanding of other people's lives and ideas and we were filled with admiration of the hardy, plucky, patient people who pioneered that country. In Dunedin there is an Early Settlers Hall hung with portraits of the pioneers. What fine faces – men and women. One would just have liked to have had portraits of them when they went there – to compare.'

Before returning to conclude their time in New Zealand with a further stay at Thames, Charles had an alarming experience which, to his relief, was not shared by his wife. Following a car mishap, he was given a lift

Charles and Edith Murray, Thames, North Island, New Zealand (1930)

in the back of a truck, driven at breakneck speed by a young fellow who had his girl in the cab. The road was steep and dangerous with many bends and, on one side, a heart-stopping drop. 'But,' recounted Charles, 'the young beggar took us up in top gear and only hooted once. I had the scare of my life as I feared he might get cuddling the lass and take his eye off the road. However, we got safely to a mining town where we got a car for the final 30 miles in the dark. It took me days to recover and I wouldn't do it again for all the money in the world.'

Back in Thames, Charles learned in a cable from his son-in-law that he and Edith, George and Bella "were all grandparents," following the birth of a son to Douglas and Peggy Walker. Impatient as the Murrays must have been to resume their world tour, especially since the next leg would re-unite them with their son and his wife, Norah, now resident in Tokyo, they chose to remain at Thames as long as time allowed. They were reluctant to bring to an end the companionship, but lately established, that had so enriched their lives and that of their aunt. Summing up the visit, Charles wrote to William Will: '... it was a happy meeting. The poor dear thought we would be much too high and mighty for her and that we would only stay a day or so. We stayed four and a half months in a very uncomfortable hotel and my wife spent every forenoon and I every afternoon with her. Man, the talks we had about her native Birse. She... had lots of interest to tell me about my mother's people.'

Charles and Edith had a further reason for delaying their departure from New Zealand. They sought 'to evade the typhoons and the rainy season' that might disrupt their voyage. From Auckland they took ship for Sydney where, after a wait of ten days, they boarded a Japanese vessel. 'And very comfortable we found her,' comments Charles. 'We called at Brisbane and Thursday Island, the latter a pearling station, about 70 pearlers in the harbour, the divers Japanese and Chinese. The diving is really for the shell which, for buckles, buttons, etc., fetches £120 a ton. The divers get any pearls found as a perquisite. Then on to Davao and Manila. Hong Kong next, a beautiful harbour and fine modern town. Then on to Japan. We sailed through the Inland Sea in perfect weather. It was too lovely for words – perfect fairy land.'

'... our boy... met us at Yokohama – a happy meeting. We are lucky people to have for an only son a straight clean lad who has never given us a moment's worry... The young folks... had one pleasant surprise waiting us – they expect the first child in a few weeks...'

'Before you get this,' Charles wrote to daughter Peggy,' we hope there will be another grandson here. It will be amusing to see Bill changing "hippins".'

Continuing his travelogue, Charles reported to George Walker: 'We trained to Tokyo. Bill could not put us up so we stayed at a Japanese hotel for two weeks and then had the great luck to get a house next door to him. We borrowed some furniture and bought some. The place had been occupied by Russians and was filthy. It had to be all colour washed and scrubbed and re-scrubbed and seven loads of dirt removed. Now we are quite comfortable... Edith and I spent a week-end at Nikko, a great show-place for temples and shrines, a beautiful spot in the mountains 90 miles from here.'

The Murrays anticipated remaining in Tokyo until the end of March 1931, when they would start for home, journeying eastwards. 'We have booked our cabins for Canada and sail on the 26th inst.,' Charles wrote to Alex Keith. 'It will be good to get on a British ship and get decent food again. I'm afraid we don't like Japan, its climate, or its people, and are sorry to leave our young people behind... '

'I am looking forward to Canada. We will break off at Sicamous, Winnipeg, Toronto and Montreal to see friends and will stay a bit with a brother-in-law in Vancouver... Hope to be back in Aberdeen by the last week in May and man, man, it will be good to be there again.' Perhaps what Charles had really set his heart on was plying his rod again "trouting on the Don".

No account of the Murrays' travels across Canada is to hand. Whether they met their targeted return date is unclear. Certain it is, however, that they were back on home ground by 6 June 1931, when both attended the Buchan Field Club's annual excursion to Strichen.

CHAPTER 20

Self Scrutiny

'... how pedestrian a bitch my muse is.'
Letter to William Will 4 December 1932

While the Murrays' son and their elder daughter were raising families, their younger girl Marris, who had gained a BA with honours in English from Oxford University in 1930, was contemplating journalism as a career. Towards reaching a conclusion, she had the shrewd counsel of her father's friend, William Will, long associated with the publishing world. The magnet of Fleet Street attracted her, but in this her hopes were disappointed and she had, like many another aspirant, to serve an apprenticeship in a provincial paper, in her case *The Press and Journal*. It was a matter of some relief to her mother that she would have her daughter relatively near at hand for a little longer.

As 1931 drew to a close, Charles wrote to William Will advising him of his own and Edith's travel plans: 'We leave here next week and will be in London for ten days or a fortnight on the way to St Jean de Luz' – a French coastal resort on the Bay of Biscay, close to the Spanish border. While the Murrays were to be in the capital, meetings of the British Association, under the presidency of General Smuts were scheduled to take place. Charles was anxious to attend some at least, in expectation of greeting old friends over from South Africa. Amongst them was one particularly close that he wanted William to meet – Sir Caruthers Beattie, Principal of Cape University. Charles continued: 'I am still a bit under the weather with bronchitis and for the first time will be glad to leave Donside. It has been a cold cheerless summer.'

Christmas Eve prompted another letter from Charles to William: '... though I have no great memories of Xmas Days as Englishers have – we had to work on Xmas when I was an apprentice but we absolutely refused to work on New Year's Day – this season makes me remember friends and so this is just a note to one of my best.'

Although Charles had thankfully sought a sunnier south, he was already focused upon home-coming. To demonstrate to William the intensity of his longing, he drew an amusing parallel, asking: '... do you remember the champion peel-and-eat-potato-man who explained his method? "When I'm eatin' ane, I'm peelin' anither an' I hae my een steekit on a third." I have my een steekit on May when I get back to the north.'

A month on and Charles remains in uncharacteristic ill-humour with life at Saint Jean de Luz, as a letter to Alex Keith witnesses: '... the place is dead. Cinemas, of course, but I can't stand them and never go... fine golf course... too lazy to go more than once a week.'

After a reference to boredom, Charles explodes: 'What an infernal waste of life this is,' and deplores the shifts he adopts perforce to pass time. His day may include 'perhaps a stroll through the streets with my wife shopping. It is marvellous how much shopping a woman manages to do wherever she is. I have started smoking again as the only thing *I* can buy is cigarettes and you must do something when you are waiting round shop doors.'

He does regain some of his customary animation when he refers to a recent foray he made just across the Spanish border from Saint Jean to Loyola, birthplace of St Ignatius. Having been conducted over the monastery which saw the birth of the Jesuit Order, Charles exclaims: 'What a place to loot if you could get away with the stuff.' The Spanish revolutionaries had just declared their intention of suppressing the Order.

The Christmas season lately past perhaps prompted mention of "Aul' Eel" in a letter of Alex Keith's to Charles, who responded with his own recollections of yule-tide exploits. 'I can remember,' he wrote to Alex, 'the shooting match at the smiddy for a plough on that day and also a barrow rowin' on the market stance... Clartin' doors with sowens was common, though I think that may have been on New Eel by then. My father told me how he clarted the manse door and the sowens ran down on to the door sill. The Minister was going somewhere early next day and came to the door in his stocking soles to look at the weather, got amongst the sowens and on his going back messed all the carpet.'

From Europe, as they had done from South Africa, the thoughts of Charles constantly reverted to Scotland. He seized eagerly upon scraps of news from home. Well aware of this, Alex Keith kept him fed with items he knew would be of particular interest: the passing of old friends; the water level in Don; reference to his beloved Bennachie which brought the response: 'I am satisfied the best view is from the brae in front of the Brig. You get the three taps beautifully but there is another good view from the side of Don, between Castle Forbes and Monymusk.' These images must have been indelibly registered upon the eye of memory.

Charles Murray enjoys 'a round on turf'.

On their return to Scotland in the late spring of 1932, it must be assumed in the absence of information to the contrary, that the Murrays resumed their regular pursuits. For Charles this would have meant sessions of the *Sit Siccar Club*; rounds on the golf course, at Cruden Bay perhaps; days on the river with rod and line. Then there was the Annual Excursion of the Buchan Field Club which that year took place on 20

August. Gathering in the *Palace Hotel*, Peterhead, members first visited nearby Inverugie Castle, before proceeding to an inspection of Ravenscraig Castle and its neighbourhood.

'A clean fish on': Charles Murray displays a fine catch.

In early October, somewhat in advance of their usual exodus, the Murrays left once more for Saint-Jean-de-Luz. Mention of his health suggests that Charles was seeking warmth. A letter of his to William Will indicates that the latter has made reference to the former's "translations"; "paraphrases" would be a more accurate description. This brought illuminating comments from Charles on his own verse writing.

'Translations are interesting to do. They save having to think out something original and it is amusing hammering and filing and trying to fit other men's ideas into Scots, but I can't think the result can be of interest to anyone else.

I did once think of having some of them and a few other scraps printed privately – just a few copies – partly so that I could then tear up my typed drafts and save my heirs having to do so and partly to see what they looked like in print. When you see a thing in print it has a fresh impersonal look about it and one can pick out weaknesses better and perhaps if I had these things off my hands in this way I might by then have a new interest in trying other things… I think I will send you a batch of the things I have and you can say what you think about them. You can be perfectly frank as I haven't the slightest conceit about my own things and if you damn them utterly I won't mind in the least but just say: "Well, I thought so"… One of the things that has put me off writing or trying to write verse is that I have no one to pass an opinion on things and I always mistrust my own judgement. So far is this the case that I kept *The Whistle* by me for months, uncertain if it had any value or not.'

The subsequent exchange of letters between the two makes it clear that Will's evaluation was positive. He had sought to stir Charles up "to start rhyming again," and that was the way the wind blew. 'I have got a bit interested again,' continues Charles, 'although a few weeks ago I had almost made up my mind I would never do anything more – felt I couldn't, had lost the knack and had no ideas left.

Anyway I have been working on a simple homely country subject and enclose the result. I doubt if it was worth doing but it was amusing to be hammering and filing and fitting at words again… You would be surprised if you saw the sheets and sheets I have scribbled to get this thing to this stage and you would realize how pedestrian a bitch my muse is. The only thing I ever did that came easy was the lines in the "Gravedigger" (*A Green Yule*) "Bring them alang" and because they came easy I doubted if they could be any good…

By the way I came on another scrap done many years ago, *The Lad Without a Name*, not worth preserving but just for the sake of tidying up you might get it typed so that I can preen it on the others and forget it.'

Nearly a month passed without a reaction from Will to the verses Charles had submitted for his scrutiny. Charles tried again on 1 January 1933. Having first extended New Year greetings, he mentions current financial "tremors" in South Africa that might reduce them to penury and "porridge". 'Well, well,' he shrugs, 'there is aye something, which reminds me I sent you a first draft of some verses which brought no comment from you. I expect you thought them such rot that the best thing was to ignore them. I expect you are right but still they give *I* think a bit of a picture of country life as I remember it. I don't think I can make much more of it so I enclose what probably is the final form for you to see. You might send it and the other back and if you care to make any suggestions so much the better.'

Will's response, when it came, must have been favourable. The next we hear of the "verses", entitled *There's Aye a Something*, is that they have appeared in the *Aberdeen Press and Journal*, the city's morning newspaper, of Thursday, March 16 1933, prompting unprecedented demand. Extra editions were required and subsequent reprints in the sister paper, the *Aberdeen Weekly Journal*. "Hamewith" had broken his long silence, proving that he had lost nothing of his creative gift. The humour, the characterisation, the precision of detail, the unsurpassed choice of word and phrase, the fondness for contrast – all are there, acclaimed by his North-east countrymen with delighted recognition. Self-imposed exile, albeit only to Europe, had again brought images of home coursing through his mind in a rich and genial flood.

The poem treats of the single flaw – "the stob to the rose" – that mars an otherwise amicable marriage of opposites: "She's great upon mainners – an' Sandy has neen." Something of the flavour can be caught in the last verse:

> To haud them oonhappy would hardly be fair,
> To ca' them ill-marrowed would anger them sair;
> There's lots o' waur bodies, she'll freely alloo,
> He's hearty an' kindly, baith sober an' foo;
> He grudges her naething, be't sweeties or claes,
> An' has for her hizzyskip clappin' an' praise.

She's busy the but as a hen amon' corn
Gin noses need dichtin' or breekies are torn,
An' ben when the littlins need happin' or help,
To kiss or to cuddle, to scaul or to skelp.
They're like her in looks as a podfu' o' piz,
But dam't there's aye something – their manners are his.

Charles Murray's homage to his birthplace took another form than words. Early in 1933, in a letter from France to George Walker, he broached the topic of acquiring a piece of land by Alford, part of the Haughton Estate, for the benefit of his fellow-villagers. What he had in mind was neither a sportsfield nor a formal park requiring fencing, draining and landscaping. 'I have such pleasant memories of wandering in the wood as a boy that I thought the village wives and children might enjoy the same on Saturday or Sunday afternoons… a sort of picnic wood or open space. After all, even country folks like occasionally to wander amongst trees and pick wild flowers and probably summer visitors would use it in this way.'

From this intended benefaction, self-promotion was entirely absent.

'I have never thought,' he continued, 'of a "Murray Park" presented by a wealthy native like one reads about, but just a bit of woodland handed over with no fuss or mention of names.'

Before taking the matter to a conclusion, however, Charles naturally wanted to be assured that 'the Village or Parish would care to take the land' and that the purchase price was fair, observing that 'the ground… is little use for anything else.'

What the donor had regarded as a relatively straightforward transaction still took much longer than anticipated. The *Murray Park Management Plan* of 1992, published by the then local authority, Grampian Regional Council, states: "In 1935 the poet Charles Murray purchased 84 acres of land from the Farquharson Estate and presented the holding to the people of Alford. Since then it has been open to the public and managed by a Board of Trustees."

Appendix I to the *Plan* furnishes a little more information: "The exact date when the Murray Park was conveyed to the People of Alford is not clear. A conveyance from the Trustees of Charles Murray to the Murray Park Trustees is recorded in the Register of Sasines in 1948… However the Minute Book of the Murray Park Trustees records a meeting of the trustees as early as 8 April 1936 and there are records of financial accounts in the Minute Book for every year after 1936." It seems, therefore, that although the legal niceties took time to complete there was early in place a committee dedicated to realizing the village benefactor's aims.

Another, if minor, act of anonymous generosity, conceived by Charles about the same time as the notion of the park, was the purchase of a set of dictionaries to be delivered to Alford School "From an old pupil".

Besides these philanthropic schemes, executed or contemplated, Charles had other matters on his mind. His wife had cut short her stay in France to return to Scotland, for their elder daughter was shortly to have her second child, which drew the comment from one prospective grandfather to the other: 'I hope Peg will be sensible and give us a grand-daughter.' His wish was granted.

In a further letter of about this time to George Walker, Charles focuses upon the question of personal tax, shedding light on his own situation regarding South Africa. It appears that within the next year he would have to decide whether to settle in the United Kingdom, or maintain his status vis-à-vis South Africa by spending substantial periods of residence there at five-year intervals. 'Talking of "Income Tax matters",' Charles writes, 'you must remember that I lived over 35 years in one of the Dominions, that I still retain my domicile there, and have my household effects there and have been paying my taxes there, not only Income Tax but Residential Tax, so long as that existed, and I draw my pension in South Africa not in London. I just have money remitted as I want it. My next year spent in South Africa will start me on a new cycle and when I return, in say, May '34, I will have to reconsider my position and intentions. I still carry a South African passport.'

CHAPTER 21

A Grievous Loss

'... like a brother to me for 52 years'
Letter to William D Murray, 20 March 1934

Confirmation of the start of his "next year spent in South Africa" comes in a letter of 17 May 1933 to Alex Keith, written on Union-Castle Line notepaper on board *SS Durham Castle*. 'We are within two days of the Cape,' reports Charles, 'after a good and uneventful passage.' This Estimated Time of Arrival accords with a sailing date of 27 April mentioned in a letter to William Will, undated but probably of late March 1933.

Not until October of that year, however, does Charles, a self-confessedly reluctant correspondent, find time and inclination to bring Will up to date with his extensive travels over the past five months and his subsequent plans. Clearly he was glad to be back in the land to which he had devoted so many years of his life and where he had still a large – but dwindling – company of friends, many with connections in the Northeast of Scotland.

From St James, a suburb of Cape Town, Charles addresses Will: 'After a good deal of wandering, I am now back at the Cape and, as my family has gone into town this afternoon, I will write you.'

Having initially spent two months in Cape Province, Charles and Edith set off on a tour that covered 'a few thousand miles – Kimberley, Pretoria, Maritzburg, Port Elizabeth, Knysna and back here. There is some small advantage,' observes Charles, 'in having been a government servant. Though now on a pension, I get one trip a year at half-fare and this long trip cost only £10.14/-.'

At Kimberley, on the Cape Province-Orange Free State border, the wayfarers paused a day or two to see Charles's sister, before proceeding to Pretoria where for two months they minded the home of an absent ex-colleague. From that base Charles was able to resume contact with many fellow public servants. One was J J I Middleton, former head of the Financial Department, who hailed from Monymusk. 'His grandfather,' recounts Charles, 'was Inspector of Poor in Tullynessle when mine was Inspector in Alford. My father was ground-officer at Haughton when his was gardener at Monymusk, and he was born at Montgarrie about two miles from where I was born in Alford. We both wound up as Heads of Government Departments, our offices in the same building and for years we had forenoon tea together. He looks after my financial affairs in South Africa and for nothing – which suits an Aberdonian.

From Pretoria we went to Maritzburg (i.e. Pietermaritzburg, capital of Natal) to see Professor Petrie. It was delightful meeting Petrie again and his sweet little wife whose father, John Rule, was forester at Monymusk. When Petrie married her, he said he was "Lord of Miss Rule".'

In the course of his travels Charles renewed acquaintance with other Scots – from Peterhead, Cluny, Kintore, and one Sim, a botanist whose father had a farm at Strachan.

'Then,' resumed Charles, 'we went on to Addo, near Port Elizabeth where some brothers of my wife's (namely Syd and Clive and perhaps William, a retired surgeon) are fruit farming – grapefruit and oranges.' There the Murrays were joined by their younger daughter Jean and had a week with relatives, 'in the middle of the orange and grapefruit hairst,' as Charles puts it. 'My brothers-in-law will pick a quarter of a million of these this year and I never ate one. Like the story of the Scot and the Garden of Eden, I never cared a damn for oranges.

From there we went to Knysna to see some old friends. There we had one of the best days of our life motoring through a marvellous forest where they have yellow-wood trees 2000 years old.'

Having returned to the Cape, the Murrays expected to remain there until after the New Year. Charles would then be entitled to another concession fare which he intended to use to the full, journeying north again to Johannesburg and Pretoria, for what he surely felt in his seventieth year must be a visit of farewell. Funds permitting, they would set course for home via the east coast of Africa, taking a last look at Rhodesia en route. 'It is nearly 43 years since I went there with an ox wagon,' recalls Charles, 'and I would like to see Salisbury again. It is now quite a city; then it was a few mud huts.'

As he contemplates the end of his travels, no conclusion seems more desirable than "back to Alford by May to the trout." A sombre tone creeps into his letter to William Will: 'After that it will be about time to buy a plot in the cemetery. A lot of my old friends have gone since I was here last and that makes you think.' The cloud is momentary, however; humour prevails: 'Lord, Lord, what a trauchle life is!' exclaims Charles, administering the antidote: 'A man told me he saw, written on a Scots £1 note.

> "Here's anither ane awa'
> Sic a trauchle life is.
> This within the week mak's twa.
> Sic a jaud the wife is."'

Some six weeks later Charles has more sad tidings to share with Will. He refers to the 'death of a dear Strathdon friend in Toronto. We stayed with her and her brother and sisters in Canada. That is the one unpleasant thing about old age: friends drop off.' This letter is accompanied by some scraps of verse, versions rendered into Scots by Charles from the Greek Anthology, versions that had first appeared in 1926 in "Atalanta's Garland", a publication of the Women's Union of Edinburgh University. The first two are genuine:

> *The Best of Death* After Pallades
> For a' we're wae to think o' Death,
>   It brings us mair o' gain than grief;
> Greet nane for him that's tint the breath,
>   He's tholed his very last mischief.

> *After Asclepiades*
> It's guid in Simmer when it's dry to drook your drouth in snaw,
>   An' fine the sailors like the Spring when Winter's win's are laid,
> But lat a lad an' lass convene, O then, it's best o' a'
>   When cheek to cheek they tell o' love, aneth ae marled plaid.

The third is a mock epigram written by Charles in parody of the Greeks:

> *Mrs Tamson at the Sculpture Gallery*
> She saw Adonis, but she turned awa',
> "Still gie me Tamson noo I've seen the twa."

Here, as elsewhere, Charles shows himself a master of economy, conveying a scene, an assessment, a conclusion entire in a droll couplet.

Three months into 1934, when the Murrays had pursued their intended itinerary as far as Johannesburg en route for home, Charles wrote from the Rand Club to his son, voicing their profound shock at the desolating news of George Walker's passing. 'He has been like a brother to me for 52 years,' acknowledges Charles, 'and I feel his death a lot.'

The Walkers – George, his parents and his sisters – were, it will be recalled, the first family with whom Charles became acquainted on his arrival in Aberdeen to begin his apprenticeship. That Charles was absent from the country and unable to attend George's funeral must have been to him a matter of intense grief. George had been not only friend and legal counsellor but, supported by his wife, informal guardian of his children when need arose and watchman over his father's well-being.

In the wider contexts of profession, church and city, George Walker had attained distinction. A partner in the law firm, Adam, Thomson and Ross, he had become a prominent member of the Society of Advocates, acting as Treasurer. Since 1901 he had been an elder at the East Church of St Nicholas, greatly esteemed for his long, devoted service. He had also been a leading figure in relation to both the Seven Incorporated Trades and the Special Constabulary during and following the 1914–18 war. His death had come with unlooked-for suddenness on the night of Tuesday, 13 March, in his 67th year. A large company attended his funeral which took place on the afternoon of 16 March, the service at the East Church being followed by interment at Springbank Cemetery. Charles had lost his oldest and closest friend. Peggy, his daughter, had lost her father-in-law.

'We sail on the 20 April,' continues Charles's letter to his son, 'and should get home about the 5 May.' A voyage of 16 days suggests that the Murrays did adopt the East African route by way of the Indian Ocean, the Red and Mediterranean Seas.

Little documentation relating to the Murrays exists or, at least, rests in the public domain, covering the remainder of 1934. Not until two days before Christmas does a letter from Charles appear in the archives. By that time of year Edith and he would ordinarily have been six or seven weeks into winter residence in southern Europe or journeying farther afield, the pattern established since Charles retired. That year, however, the mould had been broken as he explains in the letter, addressed to William Will on notepaper headed *Forbes Arms Hotel, Alford*: 'We are trying to put in the winter in Scotland with the idea of settling down somewhere for good. I would like to see my books and pictures again after 10 years and I begin to think there is some advantage in dying in your own bed.

I am looking forward to the spring, the first I have seen or rather hope to see for 47 years. The weather may be bad but the song of the birds will make up for much.' Judging by the frequency of references to birds in his poems, Charles must have had for them a particular attachment, stemming from boyhood recollections.

Charles confesses that, unlike his wife with whom 'letter writing is a bad habit,' occupying her constantly, he is a poor correspondent. 'The older I get – and I was 70 this year – the more difficult I find it to write letters.' The obstacle might have been, not the laziness with which he frequently taxed himself, but physical incapacity.

His only grandson, Kim Walker, recalls being taught some fishing knots by Grandfather Murray: 'In old age he suffered from what I believe is a fairly common complaint among elderly Scottish males – *Dupuytren's* contracture, a progressive but painless thickening and tautening of tissue beneath the skin of the hand, resulting in a clawlike curling of the little and ring fingers towards the palm. This, of course, made knot-tying with gut (no nylon in those days) a problem for him and I remember feeling very sorry that teaching me the Blood knot – which is a particularly tricky one – was such a struggle for him.'

In an undated letter from the *Panmure Arms Hotel*, Edzell, Charles admits to Alex Keith: '... my fingers are so stiff I funk writing letters... I must stop. It annoys me not to be able to write better, but *some things* get stiffer the older you get.' There is evidence that the poet's father suffered also in later life from an inability to straighten the second and third fingers of his left hand. Perhaps he too was a victim of *Dupuytren's* contracture.

Physically impaired Charles may have been, but there was nothing amiss with his sense of fun. He closed his letter to William Will with a story featuring a Scottish friend from his South African days – Professor Petrie, a great humorist. 'He took a fellow-student to his simple home on Speyside for a holiday,' recounted Charles. 'The first morning after arrival the friend asked him where the lavatory was. Petrie took him to the door and with a wide sweep of the arm said: "Onywye atween this an' Tamintoul".'

CHAPTER 22

New Home; Old Friends

'Cauld Eild, doubtfu' o' the stranger,
Thinks but o' haudin' in the fire.'
Hamewith

In his pre-Christmas 1934 letter to William Will, Charles had spoken of 'settling down somewhere for good,' meaning "somewhere in Scotland ". It might have been assumed that Alford was to be his choice. Alford, however, idyllic as it can be, is subject to piercing frosts and Charles could not abide cold. With apologies to his fellow-villagers, he directed his gaze elsewhere. A follow-up letter to Will narrows the scope. 'We haven't got a house yet,' admits Charles, 'but have still faint hopes of getting a suitable place perhaps on Deeside. The South has the climate doubtless but, when you get old, you like to be near a few friends, though the old friends are dropping off and it makes you think.' In mitigation of his choice of Deeside, it may be recalled that his mother's family hailed from Birse, some eight miles west of Banchory on a tributary of the Dee.

An undated letter of about this period to his son indicates the focus of their quest. Charles writes: 'We have heard of another possible house in Banchory and hope to look at it this week... we were lucky to get out of the other so well, weren't we?' – presumably to escape without penalty from an agreed lease or sale. "Another possible house" might well refer to the very attractive Mount Street property, formerly named *Balgownie,* which the Murrays succeeded in purchasing and renamed *The Lythe* the haven. Although their date of entry has not been determined, they were certainly in residence by 20 July 1935, the day of the Buchan Field Club annual excursion when their attendance and home address were duly recorded.

Built about 1852 to the order of Aberdeen surgeon, Mr Alexander Thom, the house could boast a distinguished resident prior to Charles Murray in Lord Kitchener who, from time to time, lodged there as a guest of two aunts of his. Location and design, however, not pedigree had determined the new owners' choice. South-facing, with a pleasant outlook across tree-clad slopes towards Kerloch and Scolty, the handsome two-storeyed dwelling of diverse granites is set in ample grounds where beech and monkey-puzzle stand sentinel. Along the southern boundary of the property lay a tennis-court, in the recollection of the Murrays' grandson, neither very level nor much played on, however.

The Lythe, Banchory, from 1935 home of the Murrays in retirement
Author's photograph

At the west side of *The Lythe* were outhouses and what Edith termed her "sitooterie" or summer-house. Behind the residence rises a building incorporating servants' quarters and what still goes by the name of the "coach-house" where the Murrays' car was garaged. Along the length of this block, in their time, there ran a loft, fragrant in autumn with the smell of stored apples.

In her South Africa days, Edith Murray had been keen on gardening and this interest she pursued in her new home, cultivating fruit and "exotic" vegetables such as asparagus and sweet-corn. Her grandson recalls visiting *The Lythe* as a youngster and remembers his grandmother as a somewhat strict taskmistress. The eldest of the eight Rogers girls, she had kept her sisters on a tight rein. Her grandchildren she required to carry out domestic duties to an exacting standard to earn the freedom of a "fabulous" garden with trees to climb and tree-houses to exult in. One of the tasks imposed – unbecoming a boy, thought Kim – was gathering lavender to give fragrance to the linen before it was carefully folded and stowed away. In tying up parcels she was precise too. No deviation was allowed. The wrapping paper had to be cleanly creased; the string – "proper" string – had to be tied professionally, no skimping on knots. No question, Edith Murray was "quite a dominant personality".

From the nature of his employment over the years, Charles, and subsequently his family, had been somewhat nomadic, occupying a succession of leased premises, Public Service quarters, hotel and club rooms, rented accommodation. Never, until he acquired *The Lythe*, had he owned property. After a few months in residence he began to realise the drawbacks. 'It is not all to the good having a house,' he writes to William Will. 'We have been unfortunate in servants and just now have been without any for three weeks and my wife practically a cripple with what I suppose is rheumatics.'

A year later matters had improved but little as he reveals in another letter to Will: 'We had a thrang summer.' So hospitable were the Murrays that they felt they could not turn away the stream of visitors, both family and friends, that arrived. Having had for most of the time no cook, Edith was quite worn out catering and only too thankful to seek respite at Harrogate where she took the waters in a successful attempt to combat rheumatism. If Edith improved, Charles unfortunately contracted the condition. Harrogate he classed: 'a fine place, but full of old wives each with either a hoast or a hirple.' That the Murrays were near their son and two of Edith's sisters there was, however, a bonus.

Their younger daughter, Jean, had been in South Africa throughout the preceding year and showed no inclination to return to Britain. Instead, at the request of Edith's retired surgeon brother William and his wife, a childless couple, Jean had travelled to their grapefruit-growing estate near Port Elizabeth to be a companion and to raise their spirits. In this, apparently, she had succeeded. She was, according to her father, 'living meantime in luxury and revelling in the heat.' Not until mid-November 1938 did she return to UK where, to quote Charles, she was 'doing some odd work for the BBC.'

He, on the other hand, was virtually confined indoors, a prisoner of winter. From Provost Burnett of Banchory, a close friend, he had received a thoughtful birthday gift – 'a load of peats, a great treat!' He

Charles Murray in front of *The Lythe*, Banchory

admits: 'I take it very easy these days. Don't get up until the day has got a good start and then just *clock*[1] about the fireside.' He was not short of company, however. Always an animal lover, especially of white cats, he had at that stage 'five cats and two puppies' but, as he writes to Alex Keith, he had higher expectations: 'I am in hopes Pat Duncan, the next

[1] brood

206

Governor-General of South Africa, will come north this month or next when he comes home. If possible I will collar him for lunch so you can meet him. He is a fine chap but terrible *dour*[1].' Lunch was duly arranged for 12.45 pm on February 2nd in the upstairs lounge of the *Palace Hotel*, Aberdeen. In addition to Charles, the party welcoming the returning exile included Dr Tocher, Dr David Rorie and Alex Keith. But for the absence of William Will, Charles's cup of happiness would have been filled to overflowing.

Patrick Duncan – later Sir Patrick – was one of a not inconsiderable number of Scots who rose from modest beginnings to positions of authority in South Africa. Son of a tenant farmer of Fortrie, Banffshire, he had shone at the village school, gaining a scholarship to George Watson's College, Edinburgh, before going on to study at Edinburgh University and Oxford. He entered the Colonial Service in South Africa, becoming Colonial Treasurer of the Transvaal in 1901, when Charles Murray was beginning his climb up the ranks of the Public Service. In 1903, Duncan was elevated to the office of Colonial Secretary, assisting in the restoration of civil government in the aftermath of the Boer War. He supported the union of the four provinces and in 1910 won a seat in the first South African Parliament, serving in the House until 1926, apart from one year, and holding a number of ministerial posts. While he opposed segregation of the races, he believed that European influence should be dominant in the country. In 1937 he was appointed Governor-General and favoured South African participation in World War II. The paths of Charles and Patrick, born not 20 miles from one another, are bound to have crossed in the discharge of their duties in South Africa, mutual regard ripening into lasting friendship and good-natured contests on the golf course. A recording of that February 1937 lunch would have made entertaining listening.

So much for the projected gathering of 'the lads of the village,' as their host termed them. For a portrayal of Edith and Charles in domestic circumstances, we are indebted to a Murray kinswoman, Mrs Chrissie Laing, late of *Mill of Kintocher*. She recalls that they had two servants at *The Lythe:* Janet Smith, their maid, and Horace Farquharson, gardener-chauffeur, formerly in the employ of Charles Spence of the *Forbes Arms Hotel*, Bridge of Alford. In young Chrissie's eyes, the liveried chauffeur

---

[1] sullen

appeared large and imposing, even forbidding. She remembers Janet, whose parents lived in a cottage next to Gallowhill School, and Horace accompanying Edith and Charles Murray on visits to the *Muir of Alford* farm where Chrissie lived with her brothers and sisters. The car would stop at the end of the approach road and drop off the 'Hamewith folk', as they were known, while Janet would carry up to the farm parcels or baskets, for the Murrays never arrived empty-handed. Horace would then drive Janet to her parents' house where both would have tea before collecting the visitors for the return trip to Banchory.

As Christmas drew near, recollected Chrissie, Charles would invite the *Muir Farm* children, much to their parents' embarrassment, to write him a note stating their choice of gift. Chrissie recalls asking for a doll and being given one of rubber, *Annabelle*, the like of which she had never seen, while one brother sought and received a camera.

Instances of the Murrays' generosity abound. Reference has already been made to the gift from Charles to the folk of Alford of 84 acres of woodland as a pleasance for their enjoyment. Concern for the common good also lay behind an approach he made to his influential friend of long standing, Dr James Tocher. To William Will, Charles confides: 'I got Tocher to interest himself in getting Corgarff Castle taken over by Government as a National Trust. It would be a shame if the scene of *Edom o' Gordon* was allowed to go to ruin. The last time I saw it, it was just a resting place for tinks.'

To cite a further, minor illustration of his charity, Charles, learning that the poet Hugh MacDiarmid, no crony of his, was in low water, sent an anonymous donation, privately questioning why he should contribute to keeping alive one who had earlier savaged not only his secret bene-factor – who shrugged off the assault – but more hurtfully the latter's closest friends. Writing to Alex Keith, one of that inner circle, Charles had prescribed for their critic 'a touch of the prob which farmers used on *hoven nowt*[1]. William Will writes that Grieve (MacDiarmid) had gone for him. Now nothing he says about me annoys me in the slightest, but I get wild when he touches my friends.'

Charles would go to no end of trouble to secure for those closest the recognition he believed they deserved. James Tocher, his schoolmate of 1872 or thereabouts, is a prime instance. Writing in 1937 to his own daughter, Jean, Charles admits: 'Talking of Tocher, I started a move to

[1] swollen cattle

get him an LL.D and after that one to get him a presentation portrait.' The latter was a *quid pro quo*, for Tocher had been instrumental in arranging the Fiddes Watt portrait of Charles, who continues '… David Rorie (medical doctor and gifted poet) usually comes along with a ballad on the occasion – he did one for mine. This time he said there must be more than one. He did one and said Alex Keith and Mary Symon and I must also do one. Mary has been ill and couldn't. I said I wouldn't but wrote a leg-pull to amuse Alex Keith.' The "ballad" *J.F.T.*, furnished by Charles, is a witty pen-portrait of the man, reciting his manifold skills and astounding feats:

Gin some aul' wylie fairmer try
To milk the pump an' nae the kye,
The Shirra kens the safest wye
   Is to remand him.
"Tak' it to Tocher," syne he'll cry,
   "Nae avizandum."

Gin there's been some oonchancy wark,
Deid horse or heifers in a park,
Jist sen' their yirnins in, an' mark
   Hoo fest wi' fushion
He'll shak' the bottle, lick the cork,
   An' name the pushon.

Statistics are to him like play,
He'll prove an average hen will lay
Three-quarters o' an egg per day,
   An' gin ye speer,
The tither quarter's chairged, he'll say,
   "To wear an' tear."

He'll note your colour, een, an' hair,
Your wecht an' hecht when tirred an' bare,
The size in hats an' sheen ye wear,
   Your clan and craft,
Till men he's measured a' declare,
   "The cratur's saft."

    ★   ★   ★   ★

He'll tell ye whisky's jist a drug,
Porter an' wine in gless or mug,
But lat me whisper in your lug,
    – Ye michtna think it –
He'll praise the milk an' pass the jug,
    But winna drink it.

The Artist's fairly got his phiz,
The very spit o' Jeams it is,
An' noo, O Lord, gi'e heed to hiz,
    Vouchsafe to Tocher
Fat maist he needs – anither niz,
    An' cure his pyocher.

This affectionate tribute appeared in a commemorative brochure and, subsequently, with an appendix entitled *On a Portrait* meant for Alex Keith's eyes only and exhibiting three ingenious rhymes for "Tocher", in the 1969 volume, *Charles Murray The Last Poems.*

Tocher featured prominently in another of Charles's abiding interests – the Buchan Field Club. Its membership embraced a nucleus of the latter's most intimate friends, not only J.F.T. himself, but Alex Aiken, Malcolm Bulloch, Alex Keith, David Rorie, William Will. Edith and Charles were among the eminent company that on Saturday, 7 August 1937, attended the Golden Jubilee of the Club's foundation. Incredible as it may seem, Club Secretary and Editor of the Transactions since 1890 had been James Tocher, the sole surviving member present at the Club's inception.

The following year Charles and Edith, accompanied by their son William and Norah, his wife, were among 150 Buchan Field Club members and guests who visited Fyvie Castle on Saturday, 30 July, at the invitation of Sir Ian Forbes-Leith and in 1939 the Club spent Saturday, 12 August, at Haddo House. On that occasion Charles had the company of his younger daughter, Jean. It was perhaps at the last of these outings that the incoming Club President, William P Milne, had heard the exchange between James Tocher and Charles Murray which he subsequently recounted with relish in the course of a tribute paid upon the former's death in 1945.

'When well into his seventies,' recalled William Milne, '(Tocher)

Charles and Edith Murray at the door of *The Lythe*, Banchory

decided to learn the piano. I was present myself when he propounded this project to Charles Murray, the poet. His old schoolfellow and life-long friend clapped his hand so kindly on the ageing Tocher's shoulder and said, "Man, Tocher, it's nae a piana ye want tae learn, it's a hairp.'" The jest is so characteristic of Charles that it brings him before our imaginations in all the depth of his comradeship and the gentleness of his teasing.

That their regard was mutual is manifest in a tribute broadcast on BBC radio a month after Charles's death. Tocher was recalling occasions they had shared, none more poignant than this, set in his long time home, 17 Carden Place, Aberdeen: 'Finally, I see him in my mind's eye, sitting at my own fireside, "wi' our fower feet on the fender," speaking of the Howe, his beloved Bennachie... of bleak rugged Callievar, and of the spring time by the Leochel Burn – speaking of the bright sunny days of long ago, when all the world was at peace.'

CHAPTER 23

Disenchantment and Defiance

'It's ill to be aul''
It's Ill to be Aul'

The months of retirement slipped by. Christmas 1938 brought carol-singers to *The Lythe*, as Charles tells Will in a letter dated 23 December: 'Tonight we will have the waits. I see a spread laid out for them in the kitchen.' While the carollers might well have been proclaiming:

> "All glory be to God on High,
> And to the earth be peace;"

the international situation was giving Charles concern. 'I like to believe,' he writes, 'the man at the wheel is doing his best and that he knows a lot more about things than I do.' The metaphor is less likely to be spiritual than political, Prime Minister Neville Chamberlain being the well-intentioned driver.

The New Year drew the admission from Charles to Will: 'I like the quiet, simple life,' and the revelation that 'a year or two ago' he had '... tried a rhyme about fishing, but it was a dud. Here's the first and last verse.' It had originally borne the title *A Teem Creel*, but was subsequently published as *The Fisher*.

> *I said in Winter "Bide till Spring!",*
> *An' dreamt o' days like some we've seen,*
> *Nor ever thocht Aprile could bring*
> *A sizzon half as bad's it's been.*
>
> ★   ★   ★   ★
>
> *A weary trauchle, Lord, is life,*
> *There's neither rizzon in't nor rhyme;*
> *Ye thole the Winter wi' the wife,*
> *Spring comes, — an' fishin's waste o' time.*

213

A close friend, Alex Keith, attributes the poem "to the late twenties," quite overlooking the fact that, prior to 1935, Charles had not seen spring in Scotland since 1888. Throughout "the late twenties," he had spent the spring (or its alternative) either in Europe or farther afield. If the poem records a personal experience, it captures Charles in an exceptionally disenchanted frame of mind. Things had been black before, but ordinarily he had been able to emerge sanguine: not on this occasion.

So fastidious a craftsman was Charles that he generally refused to let any of his "rhymes" out of his hands until he had satisfied his hardest taskmaster – himself – that he could not make a better of them. To attain this ideal he invited, indeed welcomed, critical comment on work in progress. Understandably, he resented any unauthorised tampering with his published verse, such as the BBC's broadcasting of one of his poems – rendered into the Ayrshire tongue! This effrontery, challenged by William Will, brought a letter of apology.

It was something of a surprise to Charles to learn that 'some unprinted things' of his were in Will's hands. 'I wish you would let me have back any you have. I don't like anything to be about until I am quite finished with it. *The Lad Without a Name* – you are the only one who has ever seen that as I never could make my mind up if it was worth or worthless and the *Univ at Aberdeen* is only a rough draft' (which did not pass muster). 'About the *Translations*, I would like them too as I want to have a go at them again.'

Somewhat later, as instances of what he dreaded, Charles mentions in a letter to Alex Keith how material, communicated in confidence, could be casually circulated: 'Tocher is a dangerous man to send anything to. You know that birthday rhyme (*Ae Year's Bairns*) I sent him? I found by chance he had sent a copy to Milne at Leeds, and a few days ago my sister in Africa wrote that the Provost of Turra had sent a copy to a man out there – Collie – who sent it on to Middleton (a former colleague in the Public Service, Pretoria) and he to my sister. If we don't keep an eye on him, he will have it in his *Book of Buchan* next!'

Midway through the year, Charles has some family news to relay to Will: 'My young daughter Jean came home this week and my sister and niece are here (from South Africa) until Monday. They have seen a good bit of Scotland for the first time.' Not for 20 years had Sarah Reid (Sarah Murray) set foot on UK soil. She was some four months short of her 77th birthday.

With hostilities in Europe only weeks away, Charles viewed the impending conflict with mixed feelings. 'Are we going to keep out of war or not?' he enquired of Will. 'One way or another I turned out with a rifle five times in South Africa, but now I can only look on. My wife has undertaken to put up 10 refugees if necessary though where we can put them all is not quite clear to me.'

His frustration at being merely an onlooker and not a combatant, Charles embodied in what Alex Keith terms "Murray's last lines" – *It's Ill To Be Aul'*:

> It's ill to be aul', by the years laid by,
> Sittin' safe an' saft when there comes the cry
> That tirrs the lan' o' oor stootest men,
> An' spec's the lift wi' the loons we ken;
> Still Eild can help wi' this fell stramash
> Gin't ripe the moggan, rank oot the cash,
> That's ae sure wye we can soothe the saul
>   When it's ill to be aul.'

An undated manuscript of the foregoing, included in a letter to Alex Keith, concludes with the words: '… these are anxious days. We listen in and listen in hoping for good news which is long o' coming.

Yours ever

C.M.'

If Edith was prepared to give refugees a home, Charles contributed to the national effort by investing handsomely in War Savings and paying, months ahead of demand, the greater part of his Income Tax. The burden heaviest on their hearts, however, was the knowledge that their son, who had survived World War I, was again a serving officer. 'My boy has been made a major – that ought to hurry up the war!' observes Charles in a letter to Alex Keith, undated but probably mid–1940.

A few months earlier, prisoner of a severe and prolonged winter, Charles allows his sense of impotent confinement to explode. 'Who the hell invented wireless?' he demands of Alex. 'It screeches on all day till I am deaved.' His next letter to Alex begins: 'You will, I know, excuse the pencil when you know I am sitting at the fire with a sleeping cat on my knee and without disturbing the animal I can't get up to fetch ink.'

He goes on to reflect: '59 years! last week since I left Alford (i.e. to begin his apprenticeship in Aberdeen) in the middle of a great storm,' inadvertently furnishing a date for the letter of about 17 January 1940. February brings no relief. 'I have not been over the door for weeks,' he tells Alex, '– just sit an' haud on peats and nurse four white cats.'

In a letter to his son, undated but attributable to mid-1940, Charles reports on matters domestic and war-related: '(Mother) does not work in the garden now but is out and in supervising a lot. Her garden is looking fine but there is always something she wants done and Horace (their gardener-cum-chauffeur) grudges any time off his vegetables.

The only way we have felt the times so far is the scarcity of petrol which stops us two old crocks getting about. I could probably manage to snaffle some extra but won't try as it's folks like us who ought to do without.

Nothing new here except we have a new lot of kittens. We have now four cats and five kittens. Jessie (our servant) is entertaining an RAMC tommy in the kitchen. She picked him up on the street, never saw him before. Mother says he is a fine chap. She had a talk with him.'

As 1940 proceeds, there is little information on the whereabouts and the activities of Charles. Not until September, from a letter to Alex Keith, does it emerge that Charles has had a note from his friend the Governor-General of South Africa, Sir Patrick Duncan, who has some observations to make on the verses *Lintin Lowrin' Lee*, but takes the opportunity to upbraid Charles for his protracted silence: 'A scrape o' the pen would have been very welcome too as it is a long time since I had any news of you.

What a world we are living in! What is going to come out of it all? I do not suppose you or I will see a time of settled peace again. (a sadly prophetic truth)

Here a good deal of mischief and bad blood is being stirred up but I do not think it will get out of control.'

The circumstances of the next communication to hand may raise a smile. Addressing his son in late January 1941, Charles admits he was coerced into putting pen to paper: 'I have nothing to write about really but your mother found me dozing over the fire after the evening meal and gave me orders to write you. So, for the sake of peace, I must send you a line.'

He reveals that he still maintains contact with Sir William Marris,

Indian administrator and classical scholar whose path crossed with his three and thirty years before when both were engaged on translations of Horace.

January, in the mind of Charles, was always associated with the threshold of his career. 'It is 60 years this month,' he recalls, 'since I went to Aberdeen, a country boy, to start my apprenticeship.'

Then, as in 1941, the countryside was blanketed in snow, making travel hazardous. 'We proposed going to Aberdeen last week,' continues Charles, 'to see the new Chaplin film with Tocher but the roads were too bad.'

A visit to the cinema might have come as a welcome relief in view of conditions prevailing at *The Lythe* – a house name currently something of a misnomer. 'Our home is hardly our own these days,' complains Charles, 'what with Peg's (his elder daughter's) two and their governess and little Alice and a woman in the kitchen with two little boys and a house-maid – who is now away for a week as her husband has got home on leave. I don't know how Horace fills in his days as he has no gardening or motoring. His only work is keeping us supplied with birch logs and peats. I expect he will be asking a rise of pay now the cost of living has gone up.'

Kept captive by the weather, Charles spent time trawling through his accumulated papers in search of a cherished possession he wished to entrust to a particular friend of long standing. One senses that this is a keepsake rather than a casual gift and that Charles is responding to intimations of mortality. The treasure retrieved and somewhat reluctantly given was the MS of an unspecified poem from the hand of the Angus poet, Violet Jacob, an admirer of his work; the recipient was Alex Keith. 'For fear I forget,' Charles writes to Alex, 'or get bombed or brunt out, I send you Violet's MS. "I am sweer to let it gang" to quote a line of hers in another poem[1] – but you will appreciate it more than anyone else and I have *Tam in the Kirk* to leave to my daughter. When hunting it out, I came on two local bits I took down in Strathdon from an old blind woman nearly 60 years ago.'

---

[1]   The line is from *Maggie*, a poem addressed by a sorrowing widower to his late wife on the first Hogmanay since his bereavement.

'But, O my lass! Because the auld year kent ye,
I'm sweir to let it gang!'

"Nearly 60 years ago" would refer to the early days of Charles's apprenticeship as a Civil Engineer, when he might have had survey work that took him up Donside. Be that as it may, it is significant that from his youth on he pursued this passion for Scots verse, even preserving those transcriptions for threescore years despite a nomadic life.

It was but natural that Charles should look back to landmarks in his life. He had no wish to rival his father's longevity nor did he expect to. This is evident from *Ae Year's Bairns*, the poem alluded to above, written to commemorate Tocher's and his own 76th birthdays, which fell in 1940:

> Three score an' ten the Lord laid doon
> The length o' years for laird an' loon,
> An' noo, wi' sax ayont oor share,
> *We* canna look for mony mair.
> Soon in the "Deaths" a line or twa
> Will tell the warl' we've worn awa',
> Wi' neist day in the P. & J.[1]
> A kindly par. by Alick K.;[2]
> Air warnin's[3] syne will never fash us
> Till the last trump stirs up oor ashes.
> But let me tell the Po'ers abeen
> *We* never rise till aifterneen.

The image that emerges here is of a man at ease with himself, unafraid of the prospect of death, prepared even to set his own resurrection terms. "Worn awa'" is not an ill- or idly-chosen euphemism. It suggests the gradual deterioration of a body subjected to exacting demands over a long and arduous life. As far back as his schooldays Charles had been regarded as delicate, not that that deterred him then, or subsequently, from throwing himself energetically into every activity he pursued, work or play.

For a great part of his life, moreover, Charles had been a heavy smoker

---

[1]   *Press and Journal*, morning newspaper of N.E. Scotland
[2]   Alexander Keith, author, journalist, farmer; a close friend
[3]   It was wartime and wailing sirens informed of impending attack, by bombers mainly.

of both pipe and cigarettes in the days before the threat tobacco poses to health was recognised. His grandson recollects the severe and persistent cough that racked the old man's frame. Charles Christie, his one-time colleague in the Department of Public Works in the Transvaal and the Union, has left behind a graphic memoir offering many glimpses of his chief. 'For most of us younger folk,' writes Christie, 'Charles could never do anything wrong – not very wrong! There was a sort of cult of discipleship and opinions were often accepted because they were his. If coarse Boer tobacco was good enough for him it was good enough for some of the disciples. If he kept it loose in his coat pocket there was a strong temptation to do that too though Mrs Murray was very severe on the practice!' Well might she be: she was the one who had to repair the holes burnt in the linings by smouldering tobacco in a carelessly pocketed pipe. Beyond question, this addiction to smoking contributed substantially to her husband's failing health. Indomitable of spirit and, until the end drew near, lucid in mind and utterance, he was nevertheless physically spent, content to depart.

CHAPTER 24

Beyond Mortality

'Greet nane for him that's tint the breath,'
The Best of Death

By early April 1941, Charles was critically ill. His was the mind that was straying back through distant days in far off places. He had not been admitted to hospital but was being cared for in the familiar surroundings of home.

In a letter dated 9 April 1941, responding to Alex Keith's concern, Edith Murray reveals her own foreboding:

Dear Mr Keith

Thank you for your kind note to me – he is sleeping just now and I can write a few notes – but with an aching heart – as I feel he can't get better – he has begun to wander – although he knows me all the time and is so very affectionate as if he wanted to make his going the easier for me – and yet – once when I said, 'Oh! fight it – fight it – don't leave me' – he said quite clearly to me, 'I won't leave you, of course I am getting better' – but the last few days I cannot interest him in anything – and he thinks we are in New Zealand and he is now sleeping – oh! poor darling – if he only goes with no pain!

★　　★　　★　　★　　★

With kindest regards to you both and I shall ring up if there is any improvement in his condition.
    Yours very sincerely
        E E Murray

It was not to be. The life of Charles Murray, eagerly embraced, purposefully lived, richly creative, characterised by integrity, professionalism, humour, patriotism, compassion, was coming to its close. At 1.15

am on Saturday, 12 April 1941, in the presence of his wife and daughters, Charles passed away. He was mid-way through his 77th year. The cause of death was hypostatic pneumonia, resulting in cardiac failure.

On Monday, 14 April, the *Press and Journal* carried the following intimation:

> MURRAY. – At The Lythe, Banchory, on 12 April, 1941, Charles Murray, C.M.G., LL.D., much loved husband of Edith Rogers, of South Africa. Funeral service at the Aberdeen Crematorium on Tuesday, 15 inst. at 11.30 a.m. No flowers, please.

The following day the intimation re-appeared with the words 'No flowers, please' deleted, and the instruction 'Canadian, New Zealand and South African papers please copy' added.

The press – local, national and international – were one in their praise of the man and his achievements. How could they be otherwise? Wartime though it was, *The Times* regarded Charles Murray highly enough to devote half a column to his obituary, including this personal tribute by 'P.H.':

> "That the divine spark was in him must be plain to all who have dipped into the two or three small volumes of his published verse. (But) he will be remembered with affection by many to whom his poetry can have had little meaning. During the 30 years or so before his retirement… from the post of Secretary for Public Works in the Union, there were few more vivid and human personalities in South Africa at a time and in a society remarkable for men of just those qualities. No man was more loyal to his friends or a more candid critic of those whom he disliked. He brought into the public service… a fearless and outspoken mind and a frank contempt for political jobbery and all forms of self-seeking. In the right company he was an admirable talker, with an astonishing memory for people and things and a broad and unfailing humour… Something in him that was ageless endeared him to both young and old."

In the course of a lengthy obituary, *The Star,* Johannesburg, of 14 April 1941, observed:

"Dr Charles Murray, C.M.G., LL.D.,... held the double distinction of having been at the head of the Public Works Department of South Africa during the period of the country's greatest development, and of being one of the best known, if not indeed the very foremost, of poets in broad Scots writing at the present time...

As to his charm, which the Sassenach reader as well as the Scot may feel in a rich measure, it is always difficult to define something which is made up of many subtle ingredients. His great love of his boyhood's home was a pervading quality. But so was his shrewdness and the feeling for humanity, in heroism and failings alike, which is to be found in the best of his songs...

The tinge of romance which is the general Highland birthright, a ready sense of words, contrast and rhythm, and a spice of elusive personality are other contributions to his style. Nor is daring at all lacking, as he showed when he wrote *'Gin I was God'*."

In its tribute of 14 April 1941, *The Scotsman* too referred to "the double distinction" of our subject:

"Charles Murray was not only a poet, possessed of the gifts of pictorial power, tenderness when he chose to use it, and an abundance of humour;... a master of the Scots tongue in verse... He was an excellent official and a first-rate business man, carrying out the arduous duties of his responsible post with zeal and efficiency."

The *Glasgow Herald* of the same date assigned Dr Murray "to the considerable group of writers of Scots verse that came after R.L. Stevenson, and gave the lie to the latter's despairing outlook on the future of the Doric as a literary medium... Perhaps Dr Murray had a firmer grip on the sinews of his mother tongue than any one of these. Although at times he could strain the reader's linguistic knowledge, he never wrote outwith common experience, and never outwith the traditions of rural Scotland."

The loss of Charles Murray was, of course, felt most poignantly by his 'ain folk', not only his family but his friends and close associates who were legion, and an incalculable number of admirers worldwide, wherever North-east Scots was savoured. Foremost among those devotees was Alexander Keith, personally acquainted with the poet over the last third of the latter's life and, in consequence, a well-qualified informant. Unsurprisingly, therefore, it was from his hand that there came the grateful and glowing tribute to "Hamewith" – bard and book – that appeared in the pages of the Aberdeen *Press and Journal* two days after the poet's passing.

Referring to *Hamewith*, the 1900 edition, Alex Keith declares: "We never shall recapture the glad astonishment of those who read that slim volume when it first appeared. This was art, and Scots, and poetry, flowing naturally from a rich spring, (Murray's) lines read rippling and spontaneous on the tongue like a stream in the heather; only his close friends knew how much thought, care and revision went to produce that easy, natural style. He had always something to say and he considered that it ought to be said well.

Murray's characters are always full stature... his lines... memorable... full of little pictures that are life itself to the country-bred Scot... (his work) a mellower, richer and more varied *Hamewith* after all the years. ... he had a faculty of communicating the most intense delight by what he wrote, even when it was old and familiar. Even proof-reading his poems for the 1927 collected edition I found a constant joy. So, too, was his spoken doric. People say the vernacular is harsh and uncouth. It was music on his lips, light and lilting. He never would recite his own poetry but his stories were exquisite. One despaired as much of speaking as of writing Scots like him. He was always the Scot, a lover of his own folk and his own land."

In keeping with the style of the man, the funeral service was plain and unpretentious. It was conducted by the Rev P C Millar, minister of the West Church of St Nicholas, Aberdeen, and brought together, in grief and in thanksgiving for a uniquely creative life, family and close friends, business associates from South Africa days and mourners from the Howe of Alford, his birthplace.

Following the organ voluntary and "Scripture Sentences", Rev Millar alluded in prayer to Dr Murray's "kind, gracious and lovable person-ality," making particular mention of "his great humility, his deep sincerity and his overflowing charity." He paid tribute to his work as public servant and man of letters and expressed the gratitude felt by all admirers "especially for his gift of poetry by which he so greatly enriched the literature of our Scottish land."

For the man who cherished Bennachie, no more fitting choice of praise could have been made than Psalm 121 – "I to the hills will lift mine eyes". A further Bible reading and prayer led to the committal and the brief service concluded with the benediction.

The ashes of Charles Murray were subsequently interred in Alford West Kirkyard. His grave, marked by a table of polished grey granite, lies close to those of his parents, his aunt Mary Robbie, who brought

The resting place of the ashes of Charles (1864–1941) and Edith Emma Murray (1871–1946), *Alford West Kirkyard*
Courtesy Dr Gordon L Watt

him up, and his Murray grandparents. Nearby stands the headstone iden-
tifying the last resting place of his respected dominie, Anthony
McCreadie, and *his* wife, Margaret Sharp, a teacher fondly regarded by
Charles. In typically laconic fashion he had already summed up life and
its outcome in the first edition of *Hamewith*:

> We've loved an' focht an' sell't an' bocht
> Until we're short o' breath;
> The auld kirkyard the ae reward,
> An' that we get fae Death.

Alford West Parish Church, custodian of generations of Murrays
Author's photograph

There is neither resentment nor recrimination here, not even regret; just tranquil acceptance that this is the way things are. Elsewhere in his work, as theme or circumstance determined, Charles could be fiercely patriotic, incisively but not maliciously ironic, whimsically light of touch, delightfully droll, deeply or tenderly stirred, always perceptive and precise. Lines he wrote in praise of another's poems may equally serve as lasting tribute to his own:

> Still, still they pipe, your mavises, though sair the Makkar's miss't,
> For Death that coffins a' the lave your sangs can never kist.

And what of Murray the man? The diversity of his poetical output was matched by the range of his professional skills and the manifold strands of his character. Overall, the impression that emerges is of a man intensely human, keenly alive and responsive to the beauty of creation and to the friendship he everywhere encountered, possessing a mischievious sense of humour, shrewd in business, a sound judge of his fellows, adept at building bridges between himself and others, forgiving of frailty but not of dereliction of duty, honest, honourable, unacquisitive, and unassuming. Underlying his nature was a deep-seated compassion that irradiates many of his poems, none more warmly than that touching plea for tolerance, *Still, Man, Still*, which reaches the gentle, unsurprising conclusion:

> We're maistly a' a mixture, man,
>   Like pasture on the hill,
> Whaur tufts o' girse an' scrogs o' breem
>   Raise stoot tups still.

Charles Murray is gone, but he has left behind an abiding legacy: in stone across South Africa; and in verse that will keep his name alive while Scots remain true to their heritage.